AF259262

From Czernowitz to China
and Beyond

From Czernowitz to China
And Beyond

A 20th Century Life

By
Ethel Liebman Wiesinger
Edith W. Gilbert
Margot W. Smith

Edited by Margot W. Smith
and Janet S. Linney

REGENT PRESS
Berkeley, California

Copyright © 2020
by Janet S. Linney, Claire K. Linney, Margot W. Smith

ISBN 10: 1-58790-553-1

ISBN 13: 978-1-58790-553-7

Library of Congress Cataloging-in-Publication Data

Names: Wiesinger, Ethel Liebman, author. | Gilbert, Edith W., author. |
        Smith, Margot W., author, editor.
Title: From Czernowitz to China and beyond : a 20th century life /
        by Ethel Liebman Wiesinger, Edith W. Gilbert, Margot W. Smith.
Description: Berkeley, California : Regent Press, 2020] |
Summary: Identifiers: LCCN 2020054937 |
 ISBN trade paperback) Subjects: LCSH: Wiesinger, Ethel Liebman, 1890
Wiesinger, Ethel
Liebman, Family. |
Jewish women--California--Biography. |
Jews--California--Biography. |
Chernivitski (Ukraine)--Biography.
Beverly Hills Hotel
Jewish businesspeople--California--Biography. |
Jews--China--Shanghai--Biography. | California-- Biography. |
Shanghai China)--Biography. |
Qingdao (China)--History--Siege, 1914
Germans--China--Shanghai.
Zhang, Zuolin, 1875-1928.

Classification: LCC F870.J5 W54 2020 | DDC 305.48/89240794--
dc23 LC record available at https://lccn.loc.gov/2020054937

Manufactured in the
U.S.A. REGENT PRESS
Berkeley, California
www.regentpress.net

*For the family, in hopes that they will
find their history of interest.*

Contents

Family Stories

Appendices

The Ethel Wiesinger Memoir

My mother, Ethel Liebman Wiesinger, was audio taped at her home in Charlevoix, Michigan, in 1980. This memoir is the verbatim transcription of these tapes as well as stories taken from her letters to my sister Edith. English was her second language. This is how she spoke and wrote. She lived in China during the time of foreign imperialism and had the attitudes and language of that time. She was a raconteur par excellence.

Ethel Wiesinger (1890-1984) traveled the world. She experienced the effects of two World Wars and the 1930's Great Depression. She was in business for herself for many years as an independent woman when this was an anomaly.

I've organized her story chronologically and added details from my memory of her life and historical notes (in parentheses.) My daughter Janet Linney edited it for context and interpretation.

I hope this memoir of our family will help us appreciate our ancestors' resilience as part of our heritage.

Margot Rosaly Wiesinger Smith

2021

Austro-Hungarian Empire, 1914

Since 1775, while under the rule of the Austro-Hungarian Empire, Czernowitz's culture and prosperity flourished. In the late 19th century the German language was its lingua franca due to the Habsburg's reign and Jewish influences. Newspapers were published in German. In 1900 the total population was 67,622 of which about 22,000 were Jews; less than a third survived World War II. In 1991, Czernowitz, now called Chernivtsi, became part of independent Ukraine.

Ethel Wiesinger's Audiotapes
Recorded in Charlevoix, Michigan, 1980.

CHAPTER ONE
From Czernowitz to China

Czernowitz belongs now *(1980)* to Russia; it went from Austria to Russia to Romania, which was the border country. About 100,000 people were there. We had a lovely big church, a bishop, a beautiful university and we had a beautiful temple for Jewish people.

There was a terrific immigration from Europe to America in those days, the beginning of the century. The conditions in Austria were very, very poor. We were rich because my father made a very good living. We lived in our own house, my father was a respected and prominent man. They would come to him and take advice from him, but great wealth did not exist there.

I remember going to the train to see my sister Reggie off to go to America. It was funny, the man that she was really supposed to marry died young. Regina married an Otto and I married an Otto. Her Otto was the stepchild of my father's sister.

The best people of Europe, especially in Germany, the best people left Germany because America offered so many opportunities. But when they came here to America, it began to be a class again, the very rich and the very poor. Half of the country was working like slaves for those who became rich, the Vanderbilts, the Astors, the Morgans. How did they become rich? How did they become such millionaires? It was that poor people worked for them.

Rosa and Meyer Liebman

Czernowitz, 1895

In Woolworth *(variety store),* for instance, if you made six dollars a week you made a lot of money, as much as you could make in a university in Peking, China, and the girls here worked for six dollars a week.

Growing Up In Czernowitz

In Czernowitz it was an entirely different way of life. The women didn't talk, the women stayed home. It was only men who came together and they would discuss big affairs; generally they talked about the Bible and the scribes. They talked intellectually; they thought the women would not be interested. My parents rarely went out as a couple.

My mother was neutral, she looked after us kids; but socializing herself, she was too busy. And when she had time she was tired, although they did have help. She was the mistress of the house and she had to control everything. She did not have an intellectual life because she was an orphan and she went to her aunt to live, and when she was 16 years old my aunt married her off to my father. And she thought she had to be a servant to my father. And she had one child after the other, eleven; nursing or pregnant. At 17 she had a child. When I was born she was 40 years old.

It was easy to raise me. I never had any problems or questions about my being. I grew up in a very straight line of attention and great affluence. There were no people of great affluence, like here with millions. We had a lovely house, also a corner house like mine today, huge big gardens. I was in a well-to-do home in a very orderly situation. I didn't have to fight anybody; I grew up in an equilibrium. I went to school and had no trouble in school.

Yettie Liebman

Czernowitz School Girl

The funny thing is that our children were mostly blondes. I was the darkest one with dark brown hair. But my brothers and sisters were blond, and my father had the biggest bluest eyes that you ever saw in your life. He had a blond beard. With all the wars that had been going on in Europe you never know who was really the father of children. When the soldiers of Napoleon were going by Germany to conquer Russia who knows how many Frenchmen were left over in Germany.

By the time I was a young girl, when you're a child and you play, you don't know what's going on around you, to feel. You come to dinner, you have your clothes and you play with the children and you go to school and you study; but the problems of life, to become conscious of life, the complications of life do not enter your mind. We are very selfish when we are children. If you have what we want and need, we are satisfied. Mine was not a disturbed home. I didn't know if I needed a new dress; my mother knew when I needed a new dress so I got a new dress. I never wore a bought shoe until I came to America. All my life I had shoes made to order. It never entered my mind that it could be different. I thought everybody lived that way. When I went to school I had more than the other children, shoes and things like that, but to have millionaires like they have them here today, totally out.

I was a very pampered child because most of my brothers and sisters were already grown up; some of them were even married. So I was left alone. Mother was 40 years old when I was born; my father was about 43 or 45. I was the toy of my parents. There was nothing that I wanted that I couldn't have, but I was so innocent and so naive, there was nothing that I wanted that was out of their means. So I just grew, and I went to the best schools and I was the best-dressed girl in school, so some of the children hated me. I never wore a leather shoe, only the cheviot *(sheepskin)* that was the finest kind of skin, and only button shoes; the others wore straight-laced shoes. I always had a button shoe, why I don't know.

I had a stylish blue cape with red piping and I think it cost about 9 or 10 dollars. I was the first one to have a cape to go to school with, to wear a hat to match my cape. "Aha, there she goes again." I was about 12 years old. I was not aware of it, but my schoolmates were aware of it.

Every Saturday *(the Sabbath)* we had men from all stations in life come into our house. There was a big samovar and sugar on the table. The samovar is a big pot with a chimney inside and it has charcoal around the chimney and it keeps the water boiling. And a big teapot with essence of tea, and you put it in a glass, a little bit of essence, and the hot water from the samovar. That is tea. Every Saturday night, and they would discuss the affairs of the world. I never heard a wrong word like they use today like nothing. I was in the room to hear.

They were the most interesting nights because they would sit and talk. Some of those men were students of affairs, active people, but some of them were the poor neighbors who would come in. There was one man, his name was Theodore—it's amazing what people make a living out of in Europe that we are wasting here. In every house, in our house too, the bones of the stew, the chicken bones, the meat bones were saved and Theodore had a little wagon and a horse and he would drive around in town and collect the bones. He would sell the bones to a factory that would make gelatin out of it. You can imagine how much money he made selling bones.

On Saturday, he was always our guest for dinner. He would eat dinner in our house. I don't know what his family, his wife and children ate, but father would always take him. It was always men, given that they had to talk among themselves. The men sit and discuss the affairs of the world and the Bible and the books; only men.

I was partly listening, partly inside and partly outside, and I was serving them with tea. I listened to the conversation from the time I was four or five years old up to the time that we left Austria. I must have enjoyed it because I listened.

The people who came to my father's on Saturday night met my father in the Synagogue. My father went because it was kind of a duty to go. My mother and the children rarely went to the Synagogue, only once a year on New Years. They had a gallery. We had a very beautiful temple; we didn't call it a synagogue, we called it a temple. It was very important, part of the orthodoxy. There was a very fine rabbi and a wonderful cantor, and it was more reformed. I didn't go.

In the Orthodox synagogue we would sit upstairs in the gallery with a curtain. Women don't look down and the men don't look up. They had that institution already in the beginning of time. So they knew already of temptation. *Lead us not into temptation.*

Yettie Liebman

At Home in Czernowitz

I went to school and learned history and geography, but on Saturday night they talked philosophy. And one time when I was in the 5th or 6th grade and we had geography in school and history and all the other subjects, father asked me to say if the world is turning around, why don't we turn around? And I said look, I explained it to him, I said look, if you sit on this side of the table and the table turns no matter how many times, you are still sitting on this side of the table. And those people looked at me as if I was the greatest whiz. I was about 12, 13 years old. We had geography from the fourth grade already. We took every country, every city, every river, every mountain, every forest, and we had to draw maps of every country: South America, Africa, Asia.

I went to girls' school. They had no boys in my school.We had girls' schools and boys' schools.

I read books, which my mother did not do. It was not questioned, it was expected, it was there. It was a house with reading and literature and art and music, and all these things were part of life. We were not musical but we liked music and we had to go to the opera and to the operettas, like a duty. If you didn't go you were not in the set. They talked about *Othello* and *Lohengrin* and Wagner we had to know who they were. It was part of your education. Education counted more than money.

None of those men who came into our house visiting my father, none of them were wealthy like we understand wealth here today. They all made a good living; they all had good houses. They all lived respectably. They probably had some money too, like my father, but they had not the wealth that we consider wealthy here in America. You considered education, you considered patronage; it was considered more glory than being rich. And I think the people were happier too.

Since childhood they said I was clever. It didn't mean anything to me. I didn't know. I am the way I am today, then just a girl, just a child. I was excellent in school, now when I think back how they thought of me. After six years in an elementary school we went to a finishing school and they called me fräulein *(Miss)*, Fräulein Liebman. *(This is interesting as Ethel once told of having to go to school under her mother's maiden name, Schenker, because at the time civil marriages were the only legal marriages. Children born of religious marriages (Jewish) were considered illegitimate.)*

We studied everything. When I was 15 years old we had psychology, and I was the best in psychology, history and geography, physics and zoology, somatology and biology; somatology, the study of the body. We had to paint and draw how the eye is made, how the ear is made. Every bone in the body. We had to draw the inside of the ear, the amboss *(anvil)* and the hammer. And geography. I was among the best. There is always a group of students who are the best and I was among them.

Our history professor used to say when we studied about the Mediterranean's *(Roman writer)* Cicero, he would end every lecture by saying *"Catilina must be destroyed."* And he was destroyed. Eventually he would call on me and say *Scipio Africanus*, that you cannot read. When we were tested, we had to stand in the front and recite whatever it was. And from the front row, we would help them out, you know. I was pretty good in school and I loved geography and history. I never had to study. *(Lucius Sergius Catilina (108–62 BC, was a Roman soldier and senator known for his attempt to overthrow the Roman Republic.)*

I had an older brother Joseph who was just crazy about the theater, he would have just lived in it and he never missed a show and he took me. I only went in the afternoon to the Sunday matinees because in the evening was too late for a little girl. But Joseph was absolutely crazy; he used to take me. But then when I became 11 or 12 years we had groups of girls and we all went together and we sat in the gallery for 27 pennies. And we saved our money all week to buy a ticket but it never entered my mind that I could sit in the orchestra or in a loge. We were ten, twenty girls.

Every Sunday afternoon, the classics; they gave Shakespeare more in Czernowitz than they gave it in London, all the Viennese operas and operettas particularly operettas. I saw *The Merry Widow* when I was about 13 or 14 and we'd go over and over and over again seeing the same plays, and then we'd come home and sing the arias.

Every Christmas there was one play given, *The Miller's Daughter,* a drama. Every Christmas we had to go and see *The Miller's Daughter.* I must have seen it 10 times because you wouldn't miss it. I must look up who wrote it. Lessing? Grillparzer?

About 100,000 people lived in Czernowitz. My goodness, you had to have your theater. The theater opened around September and they closed around April. Every Sunday afternoon the class would meet there. All the gallery was taken up by students, university students, gymnasium students *(preparatory school)*

Czernowitz Synagogue and Theater

The Czernowitz Synagogue was a domed, Moorish Revival synagogue built in 1873. It closed in 1940; it now serves as a movie theater.

In 1905 the Czernowitz Theatre at the city center was built as a venue for stage plays and operas for visitors; famous actors and singers from all over Europe.

We had a wonderful time every Sunday afternoon. So I knew my classics because I saw them over and over. I don't know how many times I've seen *Maria Stewart* by Schiller. She was the sister of queen Elizabeth, a stepsister. She was the older sister and she was entitled to the throne. Then Henry the VIII died Elizabeth took over the throne; Maria Stewart was married to some kind of aristocrat in Paris so she came back and started to fight Elizabeth for the throne of England and Elizabeth had her arrested and had her beheaded. A great tragedy. Schiller was putting it up that you cried; so you had to see that, I don't know how many times, on Sunday afternoon, *Maria Stewart.*

I saw *Othello, Macbeth, Hamlet, Maria Stewart,* Schiller's play about twins that got mixed up…*Die Komödie der Irrungen (The Comedy of Errors).* It is now on TV, they are giving it now and you laugh yourself silly. Because mostly he wrote tragedies, no, that was Shakespeare.

Leaving Czernowitz

Father had a transportation business. There was a big mill in the south of Czernowitz. Father had wagons, horses and drivers for transportation, not for moving only, but for merchandising. Czernowitz stores who imported things made transportation necessary, the wagons and the horses and the drivers. He was a very personable man; he went around and made friends with all the owners of the stores. The president of the mill was a big man; father transported the flour bags or whatever they had. It was a very good business that he had worked up. He gave it up, he sold out. He wanted to get out. I was 21 when we moved. They sold the

Czernowitz Ringplatz, 1900

Derfflinger Passenger Liner

house, the furniture and everything and went to China. *(Ethel told of times when he hauled barrels of schnapps from Czernowitz to Bosnia-Herzegovina in horse-drawn carts, a trip that could take several weeks. Once when he was away he lost four children to diphtheria. People of her generation tended to make goodbyes an important event, one never knew if it would be for the last time. In 1910 the Kaiser forbade Jews from selling liquor. This may have inspired him to leave.)*

I had a sister in China. She married a man who was supposedly working with the Austrian embassy in Peking *(Beijing)*. He had relatives in Czernowitz; he came to visit them, and he visited and married my sister. And my father thought that was a great luck that this great guy married my sister. It was all a lie. Dora. He took her to Vienna and from Vienna he took her to China and in China he had a small hotel. I don't know why he was in China. She was only 18 years old when Isaac Spun married her and she knew from nothing. He was visiting relatives in Czernowitz and met my sister. And she was a very, very beautiful girl.

My sister Dora was the most beautiful girl and she was blond. Isaac took her to Vienna and he took her to China. And then my parents didn't hear from her. My parents began to get letters from her, funny letters. So my father gave up his business, he had money, and he said let's go to China. At that time it was a terrific period of *mädchen handeln* where men pretend they are big men and marry girls and take them out there and make them into prostitutes. It was a big trade.

When we were in Hamburg to board our ship, my mother and I, we were in a hotel, and the date came and we had to leave on the *Derfflinger*. I did not want to go because right next to that boat was another boat, exactly the same line, but it was the *Prinz Eitel Friedrich;* he was a son of the Kaiser. I wanted to go on that boat! And I made a fuss and I wouldn't go on the boat that was named *Derfflinger,* who was a great general in Germany. And I wouldn't go on that boat and my father and mother had a terrible time. I said I only want to go on *Prinz Eitel Friedrich* because then, I could write down to my schoolmates that I had been on a boat with *Prinz Eitel Friedrich.* But if I had written that, they would have said, "So what." At that time, that was the most important trouble that I had.

When I was on the boat with my parents to China, there was a very famous German writer, Hanns Heinz Ewers, a very, very prominent writer. He was always talking to me. I was so ignorant because I hadn't seen anything of life. I wasn't dumb or stupid; in ignorance you just don't know, in ignorance, you are not aware. And that's what I was, I was very ignorant, I had seen only one life, that was my father and mother in my little home, with horses, with a dog, rats and cats, all the goats, like on a farm, and all the things that were *ungeeignet,* that is anti sanitation, mice and rats, but you cannot help it because there were bales of hay, up to the roof. Naturally the rats were coming to eat it. But all these things are accepted as a part of life.

It was a very elegant German boat, and there were very lovely people on it, and I was the only girl. So you can imagine that everybody liked to talk to me, a pretty girl at 20 years old.

And I was walking around like a queen on that boat because everybody liked to talk to me. When I was 20, I had big blue eyes and dimples. In German, there's a saying that dimples in the cheeks makes one devilish. And Hanns Heinz Ewers--I've always been a reader, you know. And I had taken along Schopenhauer, the philosopher. Because in those days, in the places we associated, if you were ignorant of literature they won't associate with you. So in order to keep your position, to have a status, you have to know Goethe, you have to know Schiller, you know Schopenhauer, you have to know all those classics in order to prove that you belong to the educated class.

I'll never forget, I was sitting there, it was a beautiful boat, I was reading *Auf Vorstellung* that is, *Sayings of Schopenhauer*. And Hanns Heinz came over to me and started to talk, and *Was lesen sie?* What are you reading? Oh, did I impress him. I made such an impression on him because, you know, everybody doesn't read *Sayings of Schopenhauer*. And they are very beautiful. From that time on he treated me differently. He thought that he could just tease me, a young kid, but when he saw what I was reading he treated me a little bit differently, with respect. He thought I was a nice little young girl.

And today, when I think back about it, I was very well read, and I was interested in the nicer things in life, reading and talking about spiritual things. There was one minister on the boat who liked to talk with me about the Bible. Well it is not a subject that everybody talks about, only people that were very interested in religion. And he would always come and sit down with a smiling face, maybe I thought I knew a lot about the Bible, but what could I know? But he always had to talk to me about it. Very lovely man. I was just another girl as far as I was concerned. I'll never forget that for another hundred years. Such a beautiful trip.

We got to Genoa, Italy, for three days. And we were in Algiers for three days because the ship needed supplies. We slept on the ship and went out every morning to see the city, Genoa. But not in Algiers; my parents were afraid they were going to steal me. We were sitting in a coffeehouse, my father and mother and I, having coffee. Outside it said, *Hier wird Deutsch gesprochen. (Here German is spoken)* And that's all they could say, as much Deutsch as they knew. So we walked in and sat at the table, mother and father and I, and at the other corner of the same coffee house was sitting a man in a very elaborate green uniform, medals and all kinds of things. And behind him were standing two men in white suits. They must have been his guards. And mother and father and I were sitting and having coffee. And one of the guards comes over and asks my father in German if I would join the men that were sitting there. It was rather a nerve. My father looked at me, and he left the coffee on the table and said, "Come on, let's go." And we left the scene and walked out.

We stopped in Genoa, Algiers, Port Said. We went through the Suez Canal into the Red Sea. We didn't know we were going to have that kind of a trip. My sister who lived in China at the time told us we had to buy tickets and my father bought the tickets and I was very good in geography. But I didn't know that we were going from Hamburg via the

North Sea via the Gulf of Biscayne around France via Gibraltar, down to Genoa. We could have gone from Austria down to Trieste in a day by train and taken the boat there. But we didn't know, so we traveled for six weeks. We left on the 10th of March and arrived on the 6th of May in Shanghai, because we didn't know. That my father didn't know surprises me even today.

A lot of people were on the ship. I don't remember-- maybe 30 or 40 in first class. I don't know how many were in the second and third class. We had an orchestra every night for dinner. It was very elegant.

After Port Said we stopped in Aden, from Aden to Singapore, from Singapore to Hong Kong, and then to Shanghai. The harbor at Singapore was indescribably beautiful. We stayed three days in Singapore. I had read the Arabian nights, *The Thousand and One Nights*, and one of the great stories is about Sinbad the Sailor, and he had adventures in Singapore. When I read of it I was about 10 or 11 years old, and Singapore was so far, farther than the sun. What were my chances to go to Singapore?

It was a fabulous trip. One had to be as ignorant as I was to enjoy the surprises that I didn't expect, unknowing. How should I know on a farm, I was so limited. Books were our entertainment. What you didn't read in a book you didn't know. Reading was always important. Absolutely. Reading was my life. we laughed about books, we talked about them. I couldn't believe it--the place of Sinbad the Sailor.

Shanghai, 1910

The Bund

Pictures thanks to LindaGoesEast.com

Shanghai Street Scene

CHAPTER TWO
Shanghai, 1910

In China, at first I was missing my friends, I had nobody to go with, and secondly I was missing the cultural life. There were not even people that my father could associate with because they were not interested in the life that my father was interested in. They wouldn't know how to talk about the Bible and the scribes all these things that my father spent his life studying. He was religious to an extent; he abided in the laws of the Bible, very religious.

My sister Dora's husband Isaac Spun had a small hotel in Shanghai, and that's where he took her. We went to see it, and my father was kind of disappointed because he thought he was a big shot. And he wasn't.

My father was 62 or 63. He had an idea: he saw the coolies carrying the loads on their shoulders and on bamboo sticks; so why don't we open a transfer company like we had in Czernowitz? He had the money to do it but my sister's husband wouldn't let him. He said the Chinese would strike and would destroy it because it would take their work away. It would not work in China. So then my father didn't like to stay there. *(Edith said that at that time most Jews in Shanghai were Turkish Jews, not Ashkenazi, so the family did not feel at home there.)*

He became a good friend of the Austrian consul, a very fine man, who said if you don't want to stay here, go back to Austria and somehow my father didn't feel like going back to Austria after he gave up his business. So he went to New York to his sister. My father was a gentleman to the manor born, and he was not used to women who were

*Dora Liebman with Isaac Spun
in a Rickshaw, Shanghai*

Lilly Liebman

soldiers. And she was a soldier. I think she was a younger sister. They didn't get along very well but she had a house; they pretended that they were getting along. My father was not a fighter.

So he left for San Francisco and New York and we stayed in China. In Shanghai, we had a lovely house; with my mother, we rented a very lovely home. I was there two years. We were invited out for afternoon tea and we had a carriage with a horse.

Social Life

China was an exciting place. I was the only girl. I went to lots of parties and everyone wanted to dance with me. And I was so stupid to show off what I knew because I didn't know anything else to show off. I used to sit and recite poetry. There is one poem that Schiller wrote that is internationally famous *Die Glocke,* the bell. It started with *Fest gemauert in der Erden Steht die Form, aus Lehm gebrannt. Heute muß die Glocke werden, Frisch, Gesellen! seid zur Hand.* And it goes on and on and on.

Living and being educated in Europe, they know in a minute when they talk to you where you belong. The nice part about that way of life was it was not a question of money, it was a question of knowledge; education. If they mentioned a famous author and you didn't know who he was it puts you right out. I started to go to the theater when I was 10 years old because I had to know, I wanted to know what was going on in the theater. I was crazy about theater.

Now here I come, a young girl to Shanghai, and we sit at a table and the men are drinking their whiskey soda, and I didn't drink any whiskey soda, I was not used to drink

Yettie Liebman

Shanghai, 1910

anything at home, maybe once in a while a little wine, and someone comes up and I say *Frisch, Gesellen! seid zur Hand,* "*Immediately laborers come to work,*" and they looked at me, I was like out of a different world. And then I had to recite it.

Today it can wake me up and I still know it, it is something that goes into your blood. I didn't bring any books to China, but there was a German bookstore, and there I got the books. But my own books I didn't bring. *"You must work so hard that the sweat must come down your forehead." "The master at the workshop pays the labor but the blessings come from up above."* You can imagine how I impressed those people.

I was the queen of Shanghai. And not only that, there was a piano. And I could sing. And I could sing all the German songs that we sang in school, which they had not heard in Shanghai and they were lonesome for them. *"Who has created that beautiful forest in the hills which is so precious" "I have to praise God for being so gracious as to build that forest that we can enjoy."* I knew them all because for nine years I sang them in school. And they all sang these songs with me because they all knew them. It would never enter their minds to go to the piano and sing those songs alone but when I was there, but how I impressed them was incredible. It wasn't because I was so beautiful or so wonderful but because I was young. There was no choice.

And I did not know what was happening to me. The people were so different. They were always dressed up. In the evening we were always in evening clothes. When we were eating alone at home we changed into evening dress. When my father, my mother, Dora and her husband, and I had dinner together the table was set beautifully, and we were all dressed and sat at the table and there was always an extra place in case somebody comes in. And somebody always came in. That was the only excitement we had.

Meeting Otto

I met Otto Wiesinger in Shanghai. We knew each other and liked each other. He was about 28 or 29, about eight years older than I was. At that time, there was no such thing as dating and going out. You had *ein Verehrer,* an admirer. But you still went with a chaperone. In Shanghai, he used to come to the house; we used to go to the German club to dance. There was no such thing as regular dating like they date here now.

When I came there I was a sensation because I was the only German girl there. They were taking bets: who would take me out. Otto won the bet. He really didn't win the bet; he won the bet because I had been betting with him. I quoted a sentence from one of the Schiller dramas, I was out of school and I had remembered everything. They were mostly college, university men, educated men there, and what did they care what Schiller wrote or not?

It was just perchance, we were sitting at a table and somebody quoted a sentence out of a play by Schiller; he said it was from Goethe. I said "No, sir, you are mistaken, it came out of Schiller's *Wallenstein.*" And they looked at me and said who am I to quote them. "Yes, from Schiller's *Wallenstein,*" and they started to argue about it, and I said, I'll take a bet. I knew, because we had read these plays in school. And Otto took the bet. He said it's from Goethe or some other person and I said *Wallenstein* by Schiller, and I won the bet. He said what shall we bet? And I said I'll bet a bottle of champagne if I lose, and I won Schiller's *Werke* if I win, because I didn't bring any German books to China. I won, and I still have the books. The complete works of Schiller. I was just 18 or 19 years old.

I only got acquainted with Otto when he lost the bet. That brought us together. He invited me for a ride in a carriage. That was something special. He came over to the house and asked if I would take a ride in a carriage, it was a ride of about two miles around Shanghai. The club was on the Main Street, like the Bridge Street here *(in Charlevoix),* by the German club, so everybody was standing on the porch of the German club to watch me drive by with him in the carriage.

There was never a day when there wasn't some kind of excitement, particularly when we lived in China. It was going out to parties, giving parties, meeting different people. There was an international community in Shanghai, and you had to meet people and you had to be nice to them whether you want to or not because everybody was practically a representative of his country. It wasn't like you do as you please, you didn't do as you please. You made it exciting because there was not much choice.

Williamsburg, New York, 1912

The Bridge

Townhouses

CHAPTER THREE
New York, 1912

On the boat to America I traveled with the governor of the Philippine Islands, when the United States ruled the Philippine Islands. And there was a very lovely man, a governor, and he was on the same boat with me coming to America. And they were playing on that boat Chinese checkers, and I had never seen Chinese checkers. So he invited me to play a game of Chinese checkers; I must have played it before with somebody else because I knew how to play, and I played Chinese checkers with him and I won. I never wanted to play with him again because I thought I would never win again and I didn't want to lose my reputation that I was a good checkers player. He was such a nice man. He told me about Reno. I had never heard of Reno where you get divorces, and you get married again. He taught me a lot about the United States.

Everything was a let-down in New York. It was a terrific comedown, a comedown from a home in Europe. We were not millionaires, but we were a well-situated middle-class family. We had certain rules by which we go, to go out in the evening alone was impossible. If anyone found a girl on the street, she was only one kind of a girl. Decent girls did not go un-chaperoned in the evening on the street. And I come to New York, and they run around like wild. I had to learn all these things.

I remember when I went with my aunt to buy my first dress. I never had a bought dress. They were all made to order. You couldn't buy one in Shanghai either. They didn't have any shops for dresses. So, I come to New York and my aunt takes me to a place and I buy a navy blue dress

Ethel Liebman

When Yettie Liebman arrived in New York in 1912, her Aunt told her she could not be Yettie in America, so they chose the name Ethel, and she was known as Ethel ever since. (At that time, Ethel Barrymore was a famous actress.)

that had a little collar and the collar was embroidered in red scallops, I fell in love with the dress and I bought that dress. But the skirt was only basted to make it longer or shorter, but I didn't know that, and I wore the dress basted. My aunt would always say to everybody "She's so dumb. She doesn't know how to sew her hem." She didn't realize that I didn't know about basting.

The New York Family

In New York I had to get used to my cousins. I had cousins who were my age, but they did not accept me. To them I was the ignorant foreigner. The men you casually met, they looked so strange out of a different world. And to dress for evening at dinner and have the Chinese wait on you? There, you went to the kitchen and you helped yourself. It was a plain, common everyday American life.

And you had to get used to it. It took a lot of adjustment. They always introduced me to their friends because I could talk only English to them, because a greenhorn didn't talk English *(They spoke Yiddish)*. A greenhorn had to suffer for years in New York or wherever they were to learn the English language.

But I had had English in school and then I had a teacher in Shanghai who taught me English. I didn't speak a perfect English. I spoke that people could understand me. I could make myself understood very well. And I said "Morning" and "What o'clock is it?" and they laughed, I was the laughingstock. They said, "Oh my, there is a girl coming from another world and she speaks English, how funny that is."

My aunt and all my relatives were there, my father's sister, Bubbi, *(She was known as Bubbi, elder female.)* my Uncle

Herman. Herman was such a fine man. He invented these ice cream tables, the machinery, and became very wealthy. And that was the most important thing in their life. They were both uneducated.

Ice Cream Parlor Furniture

When they opened the Williamsburg Bridge that opened up Brooklyn, immediately they began to build. If you go across the bridge into Williamsburg, when you come out of the bridge you come into Williamsburg. There was one section where they built brownstone houses just like they have in New York in the upper section where the elegant lived. They built on Ross Street a row of houses like in New York in the 1860's and 70's; they had those English houses where you go up steps, and then you had this parlor and you had the dining room and a pantry. Downstairs you had the kitchen and upstairs you had the bedrooms. And they built those houses.

My aunt, my father's sister in New York, when they became so successful she was one of the first to build one of those houses across the river in Williamsburg. She was the first one to run down there and buy a house. When we came, we rented an apartment so we could be in walking distance from our house to her house. We had a lovely apartment in Brooklyn. She was a fantastic woman.

Regina Liebman Goldberg

My sister Reggie and Otto Goldberg first lived in Harlem. At that time, Harlem was being built up, and Otto was a plumber. He had his own plumbing business, and he had jobs from buildings that were going up. But then, it turned black, the blacks began to move into Harlem. So Otto moved to Long Island, to Arverne, a place just like Charlevoix, and he opened a plumbing business there. They were very successful,

But then my sister was funny. She had three boys and a girl and she always had pains in her side. The doctor who treated her said she had a bad appendix; you must take care of the appendix. And she was afraid. When the big flu was here in 1918 after the war, after the First World War, she got an attack with the flu and the appendix and died; 48 years old, and left Otto with four children *(Albert, Jules, Nathan and Marian).*

I only associated mostly with my aunt, because after all she was older, and she had more compassion. My aunt didn't like my mother because my mother didn't clean the house as much as she cleaned hers. My mother never had cleaned houses. When my mother was at home with her aunt they had help. When she was married in Czernowitz they always had help to clean the house; she never washed the laundry, she never mopped the floors, she never made the stoves. The girl used to come in at 5:00 in the morning to every room that had stoves and she would lay the fire so that the children would get up in a warm room.

And this woman didn't understand all that and didn't want to learn, so there was always a kind of distance. But she always came and visited us, and my father never went to her house. Never, I don't know why. He felt no friendship. We were just foreigners, greenhorns. They were already born there in America, they were Americans; and who are we? They did not know whether I was an educated girl, or a simple girl, I did not know the language that well that I could argue or talk, I talked a different English, not American.

I didn't understand them, I was too young to go into analysis to understand why they don't like me, I was a foreigner to them and they didn't understand me. They were in high school. One was in university studying to become a teacher, which she did. They looked down upon me as the poor immigrant. There was no getting together; I didn't know how to meet them or they me.

Ethel Takes a Job

They wanted me to go and look for a job in a factory, like everybody worked. There was nobody sitting home. I was afraid to go. I didn't know why I didn't want to go. My aunt and her children said "What do you mean, sitting home doing nothing? Why don't you go to work?" And they were right.

I went to work one time, and it was very funny how it came about. One of my cousins took me to Macy's, and we went from floor to floor to see the different departments. And we came up to one floor, the fourth or the fifth, and we looked around and she took me to the embroidery department. They had a teacher for handwork, and there were women sitting and learning how to embroider, how to knit and how to do those things. They had probably a very efficient teacher who taught them.

And Fannie said to me, "Come on, I'll take you to where they do the handwork." So, I go over and I look at them and say "My god, that's terrible." She says "What's terrible?" I say "They don't know how to embroider. They don't know how to knit." She looks at me and says "Can you do that?" I said "I can do it but I don't do it so terrible. I do it better." She looks at me so surprised, "You can embroider, you can knit?" Well, I said of course.

It was so natural to me. All my life from the first grade on we were taught to knit and embroider. So, she said "Let's buy something and let me see how you can do." Fannie was married already and been divorced already. She was a very experienced cook, which I did not know then. I did not understand these people. So, we went ahead and we bought a pillow and all the material that I needed and I took it home and I started to embroider. And they were aghast. They never knew that I could do such a thing. And I didn't know that they didn't know.

They said if you can do that work you ought to get a job. So she began to look up in the newspapers for jobs for me. I did not know what a job meant but I said "All right."

New York City, 1912

Market Day, Jewish Section

Macy's Department Store

There was a job, embroiderers wanted. Well, she said. "That's for you. There's a job for you." I said, "All right. but I don't know how to go, where to go, what to do. Come with me." So Fannie went with me.

The embroidery place was a factory that embroidered gowns for the theater and for the opera, and they made those very showy embroidered things that were the style then. Fannie told the people that I can do embroidery and I got a job. And I did not know how to go fast with these needles so they gave me a frame and gave me a piece of material to embroider and I stitched and stitched and made it as fine as I would have made it at home. And there was a forewoman, a fore lady, and she comes over and says "You better hurry up, this has to be out very soon. You don't have to make it so wonderful."

How do you hurry up an embroidery? I went ahead and I made it. And it must have been very nice. I worked a week there and it was payday. I didn't know how much money I was going to get, and I got $18. And the other girls only got $14 a week. I was the first one and I got a check for $18. I wasn't surprised. I thought it was coming to me. I didn't know anything about wages, I'd never worked for wages.

So I come home, and on the way home I had to pass by Auntie's house. And I always used to go in. We didn't live far away from one house to another, so I said I'll go in and say hello to my aunt and show her my check. I come in and say "Hello Aunt Bubbi." She said, "Where do you come from?" I said "I come from work." "Oh, you come from work." I said "I got paid today; I have a check." She says, "Well, how much did you get?" I said "I got $18." She said, "Don't you dare lie to me." I didn't know that I was lying to her. So I take out the check and give it to her. She nearly died. *(They had her sewing seed pearls on satin gowns.)*

Those were the days when they paid $10 a week. Loom work only paid the girls $10 a week. I don't know if they had the unions already, people worked for very little money.

I enjoyed sitting and embroidering. And there was one girl, an Italian girl who worked with me, she was the only one I could talk to. I could talk to her in my language, and she told me that she was a schoolteacher in Italy. And she came back and she was embroidering for $14 a week. And I came in and got $18. I didn't tell the girls that I got $18 check because I thought they all got $18.

I worked there three months. Then they closed, slack time. Slack time? What's slack time? They closed the factory; they stopped working. They finished the jobs for the theater, they closed the factory and then in three months or six months, when the opera comes back they open again and employ people and make the clothes that they need for the new things. I didn't know what slack was. I worked for about six months and never worked again.

I wanted to go to college to become a doctor. I matriculated to be in college in New York, a New York college. They accepted me. I went first to school to translate my knowledge from German into English, and I passed. The school that I went to, the principal said I had to take German too; I had to take a foreign language. I said, "I don't have to take a foreign language, I speak German." He dealt mostly with Russian Jewish immigrants. So I didn't listen to him, to take German, and went to take the Regents Examination and I passed every subject. And I had

Yettie Liebman's Matriculation Card, 1914

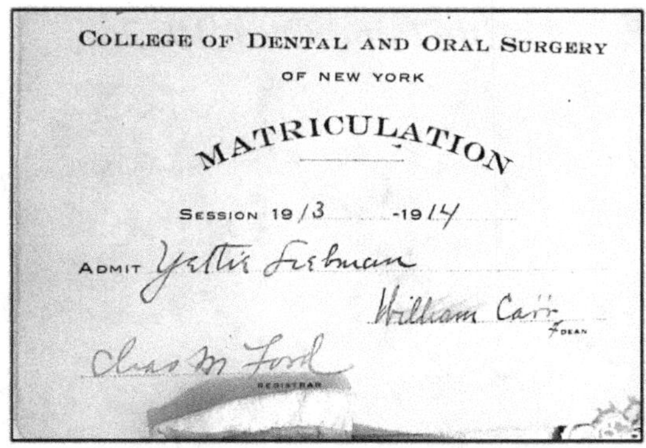

only nine years of school, but I was so drilled in knowledge, in literature and in the fundamental things of education, history, geography, and all these other subjects. So I went in; he laughed that I would go in to take the examination, he said that surely I would not pass. I passed with the exception of English. And they accepted me. I still have the card, my matriculation card in college. I didn't go to it.

After working, I went back to that school to learn English so I could translate what I knew in German, and I wanted to go to college. I waited for college to open, and I came in and I showed them my registration that I passed except English. There was a very nice man sitting there and he said that the English I could study during the year that I go to college. I never went, but I have the card.

And then in 1913 Otto came on a visit, a trip from China to Germany, and he visited us. And we were again feeling we were in an equal circle. We spoke German mostly; he didn't speak English. My parents liked him, but they didn't like him to marry me. *(He wasn't Jewish.)* He was a very fine man. He stayed a week or so and went on to Germany. And he

Ethel and Otto, 1912

had three months vacation and that's when he resigned from the company that he worked for and started to prepare to go into business for himself.

And then his misfortunes began because in 1914 the war broke out. He was already in China. His orders being manufactured for shipping to China were caught in Belgium in German ships and confiscated. He lost all the money and he had no merchandise for his office.

CHAPTER FOUR
Being German in China

When the European countries came they took over by force parts of China. England was the first one, they took over Hong Kong that they still have. *(1980)* They took over the entire coastline in China where all the ships used to come. The first war that England had with China they call the Opium War. When Queen Victoria took over India and Disraeli the prime minister met Victoria, he took her hand and kissed it and said, "And now you are the Empress of India." Victoria became Queen of England when she was 18 years old in about 1836 and she really knew nothing. They only took her because they had nobody else to take. Made her Queen of England and then they called her the bloody Victoria. The poor kid did not know what was going on in politics. She was the daughter of a British duke.

Then, the diplomats and the politicians, they ruled the country, and it was going into that industrialization that was all over the world, including England. So when she became the Empress of India they had to exploit India, they had to use it. They dumped the things they manufactured in England, they sold it to the Indians and the other countries too. India was very primitive, and they could get rid of their merchandise. The big British concerns made offices in India, and then they wanted to go to China and then to Japan. They began to open offices in the Orient.

The German Kaiser was always very jealous of England. In 1910, Kaiser Wilhelm's mother was the eldest daughter of Queen Victoria. Queen Victoria was the grandmother of Wilhelm II.

Shanghai in 1912

Postcard: The Nanking Road, Shanghai

The first war that England had with India was theOpium War *(1839)*. They grew a lot of opium in India, so they wanted to send the opium to China. The Chinese didn't want the opium, but they were forced. England won the war because China didn't have any warships, they didn't have any ammunition and so they lost the war and England got Hong Kong and the coast--all the way up to the end of China until it reached Japan. They conquered the coastline which was the most important line in China. That's where they got all the things that they wanted from Europe, all the imports, all the shipping.

Well, they won the war, they sold their opium and China became an opium country. Most of the women smoked like mad. And of course the Chinese had two, three, four wives. And those wives had nothing to do but serve those men, to be *opiences*. They had nothing to do and were probably bored to death; for the babies they always had help, so they became *opiences*. Even when I came to Shanghai and had to employ help I had to make sure they were not opium smokers.

So England sent out hundreds of men to start businesses to import products of England, and they sent out choice people, they had to be representatives of England. Then Germany followed, and from that time on, every other nation followed the English custom. There were no white women in the Orient when they started, only Chinese women.

They had the *Boxers* in China—rebels who opposed England and opposed Germany and opposed France. When they killed the German Ambassador in Peking, Germany considered that a reason for taking advantage, they having killed the Ambassador. And they went to the Shantung

Ubergehiemrat Karl Wiesinger

Otto's Father

Karl Wiesinger designed the customs system for Hamburg Harbor; it was copied by the United States in the 1790s.

Peninsula and they developed Tsingtau to become the nicest part of the area. *(The Boxer Rebellion, or Yihetuan Movement was an anti-imperialist, anti-foreign, and anti-Christian uprising in China between 1899 and 1901. Klemens von Ketteler (1853–1900), a German career diplomat was killed during the Boxer Rebellion.)*

So when Germans began to open offices, they also picked the finest people they could get, experienced with manners and background and vocation. They wanted to impress the Chinese; they wouldn't send out people who wouldn't fit. So this was everybody you met in Shanghai or Hong Kong and in Yokohama.

Otto's father was a very big official in Germany. He was *Ubergehiemrat* Karl Wiesinger. He was the greatest authority in Germany on customs, duties and taxes. If you read today the German encyclopedia there is the name Karl Georg Wiesinger, authority on customs, duties and taxes. *(Wiesinger, Karl:* **Die Zölle Und Steuern Des Deutschen Reiches.** *(The Duties and Taxes of the German Nation), 6.Aufl. München: J. Schweitzer (A. Sellier), 1912.)*

Once, when I went to Vienna to buy a little dress for Edith I put it among my clothes and didn't pay any duty. I come into Hamburg and show it to my father-in-law and my father-in-law nearly died. He wanted to arrest me. I didn't know these things.

The people who were in China representing the foreign offices were all chosen people. Holland was there, Belgium was there, France was there, but France didn't have a colony, they only had a section of Shanghai; their own quarters. France went to Vietnam and Siam, those countries.

Otto Wiesinger In China

When Otto graduated from gymnasium, *(preparatory school)* he was to go to London and become an apprentice in a bank. In those days one needed pull in order to get anywhere. Since his father was a high official in the German government, he got the assignment. Everybody was excited about his leaving for London, particularly his stepmother who was very fond of him and more excited than anybody else. As he was packing his valises and some friends were standing around, his mother said to him: "Now Ottl, remember, the minute you arrive in London you hire a droschke *(carriage)* and drive right to the brothel." *(She had heard something about a boarding house and mixed it up with the latter),* Everybody roared; innocently she asked; "What have I said now?"

Well, he did not get to London and not to the brothel, unless he went later without letting anybody know. A good friend of his father came next day telling them that he had a much better apprenticeship for him at Ehrhardt and Company. They were the agents for the Hoechster Farbwerke and the future is much brighter, so he unpacked and did not go to London. The Hoechster Farbwerke was in Hoechster and it is still an independent factory. Later they combined with others and formed the German dye trust *(I.G.Farben).*

While Otto was with them he was sent to Dresden for a year where he studied herbs and chemicals, He was sent to Switzerland to study the watch industry and finally back to Hamburg to Ehrhardt and Company headquarters. His apprenticeship lasted three years. During that time his father supported him. Apprentices were not paid. In fact many times they had to pay to be apprenticed. Besides working ten to twelve hours a day, Otto had to go to evening school twice a week. There was little time for play; still on Saturdays and Sundays he enjoyed bicycle rides with his friends, or dancing in public dance halls. His father and his bosses were very strict. On holidays Otto went home to Hamburg to his excited mother where everything was a great problem; to bring a friend home to lunch or dinner was a world affair.

She was a very good woman, crazy about her Ottl, but not getting along with his brother at all. Otto was only two years old when his father married her, but Walter was six and probably resented her; therefore the difference in affection.

Ehrhardt and Company was a very reputable firm in Hamburg, the owner a very shrewd manipulator. Mr. Ehrhardt was an old patrician merchant. He loved to drive through town with a carriage and four horses, but he too met with reverses. The dye agency put him on his feet. It was in the early 1900s and blue indigo was discovered by the Hoechster-Farbwerke. Ehrhardt changed the name to China Export and Import Company; that existed until the communists took over in China. I don't know whether they still exist in Hamburg. They had offices in Hong Kong, Shanghai and Yokohama. We visited Mr. Schmidt in Yokohama who was one of the directors of the firm.

After proper training Otto was sent to Hong Kong to start teaching the Chinese the use of chemical indigo, the dye invented in Germany. And he came out to Hong Kong to teach the Chinese how to use that dye. Before that, the Chinese used only vegetable dye, and you know that is a big process to use vegetable dye. You have to have a lot of vegetables. And indigo dye was invented in Germany and it covered China.

They did millions and millions in business. Indigo is used for the jeans many are wearing.

He traveled to Canton and the interior introducing his indigo. It was not easy, the Chinese were very reluctant to the change, but eventually they did accept and the firm sure made money. The manager at Hong Kong was a Mr. Grossman, a sour bachelor with whom he could not get along too well, therefore when his three-year contract was up he was transferred to Shanghai. Life was a little gayer there, although Hong Kong was rather a social center because of the dominant English population.

Otto on Horseback

Hong Kong, 1912

In Hong Kong, Otto had a nice horse that threw him occasionally; he lived with three other men in a great mansion on the hill, which was called the Men's House; each man had his personal boy, besides the cook, the cook's helper, the general coolie, the number one boy, a butler, tennis boys, grooms for their horses, human labor just did not mean anything. Otto was very well paid when with the China Export and Import Company They used to give their employees every Christmas *tantième,* which means bonus, and they were considerable.

It was not much different in Shanghai, but instead of the horse, Otto joined the German Volunteer Corps. It was quite an event when the German Volunteer Corps marched through the Streets of Shanghai. Never did a nation have so much respect as the Germans enjoyed in those days. Until the outbreak of the First World War, it was regarded as absolute fact that the Germans were the only honest ones in the world, the only decent ones, honor was the password. Well, with the outbreak of World War I *(WWI),* everything changed.

In Shanghai, it was a different life. There was nowhere to go. You go from one house to another. They go to a bar, they go to a bar and get drunk. So they had to make the most out of almost nothing. One time Otto was driving, he was maybe 21, 22, years old, there were a number of other Germans, German men, there were no German women to go with. They drove around at night and they didn't know what to do so they went into a Chinese place and stole a pig. And they took that pig into the car and they drove around all night and the pig was screaming and they were laughing. And they had fun taking a pig around to drive, because there was no one else to take.

In 1913, the second three-year contract with the China Export and Import Company was over and Otto did not want to renew his contract. He took his leave that was coming to him and went to Germany via the U. S. While he was on the Pacific an English warship stopped the American boat and tried to take him off and make him a prisoner of war. But the Captain claimed the boat to be

American territory; the British had no right to enter American territory and so they let him proceed to the U.S.

In Germany he began to contact manufacturers and get various agencies, he was lucky to get the agency of a small dye factory, and after remaining in Germany about six months he returned to Shanghai and opened an office. He had artists make very clever trademarks. Trademarks were very important in the Orient. The Chinese buy mostly by trademarks, they were copyrighted, so that very merchant had his own. They were quite costly too. He was liked by the Chinese, he surely would have made a big go of it had not the war started

They had nothing in China. Everything was imported. Otto had placed many orders in Germany that were to arrive within the next months. The merchandise was shipped on German ships to China via the Suez Canal. But the First World War started *(July 28, 1914)* and all Otto's orders were confiscated by the British, along with ships in Belgium. The only things that arrived safely were fifty barrels of dyes and some Irish stoves. Everything else was lost. The ships were confiscated and he never got his merchandise. It was all paid for.

Otto had a bank account, of course, with the German bank in Shanghai. At that time nobody dreamed that China would also enter the war so he left his bank account where it was. China confiscated the German bank and everything the Germans had, and so Otto lost everything he had gained in the six years that he worked and saved in China.

When the First World War broke out, communism from Russia had already penetrated to China. But the white people in China, the French and the German and the English, never mixed with the Chinese socially or in any way but business. So they didn't know that in the interior of the country Mao Tse Tung and the other coolies and the Chinese eagerly adopted communism because it promised so much. It can't keep what it promised, but the promises alone sell communism because mostly they sell it to the poor people. And the poor people don't question as long as you promise them a bowl of rice and a cup of soup.

The War In Tsingtau

When Germany declared war, World War I, Tsingtau was in German hands. They had 5,000 soldiers there and they were building up that land. The British had bribed Japan and promised them all kinds of things and Japan declared war on Germany. They had sights on the German colony. *(The Siege of Tsingtau was an attack by Japan and the United Kingdom on the German port of Tsingtau (now Qingdao) in China during World War I, 1914.)*

Germany took that land on the Shantung Peninsula from China in 1897. They were leasing it for 99 years and they made a beautiful spa out of it. They had it only about 15 years, that entire peninsula, Tsingtau. From the time they took it over until the war broke out they made Tsingtau the greatest star in Asia. Rich people from India came for the summer to Tsingtau, Shantung. They built a railroad, they built first class hotels; it was a fantastic town. Edith was in Tsingtau. I was never there. *(The German colony in Tsingtau established a brewery, that is why we have Tsingtau beer today.)*

The World War was declared in the first week in August, 1914, and in September Japan declared war on the

Germans, 5,000 Germans, and Japan was there with 40 million people at home. I met Count Waldeck, the governor of the Shantung Peninsula, in Shanghai. Count Waldeck, the governor of Tsingtau, was the most gorgeous man you have ever seen in your life, we knew him very well because he used to come into Shanghai and we used to entertain him. He would go to the German club; we were always there when he came.

So Count Waldeck telegraphed the Kaiser asking what shall we do? Because at that time the 5,000 could have either been sent back to Germany or sent into China to get them out of Tsingtau. And what did the Kaiser answer? *We are fighting to the last man.* Japan was on the side of the Allies, England and France, and Waldeck did not know what to do. He had only 5,000 men and a number of German warships: the Kaiser answered him, *"We are fighting to the last man."* 5,000 Germans against 40 million Japanese. They fought from August to October 1914.

In 1914, Otto was in Shanghai. He had money there. He had rented a building and was ready to start a big import-export business. And the war broke out. He was in Shanghai, and you know, the Germans are very romantic, fatherland people. And Otto was sitting in Shanghai had no merchandise to sell, it didn't arrive, so he joined the soldiers and sailors in Tsingtau. He joined the German volunteers and he went to Tsingtau to fight the war; the Kaiser said *"We're fighting to the last man."*

Otto and Mr. Drier were very patriotic. And they joined the German forces in Tsingtau. There were 5,000 German soldiers in Tsingtau, and Otto and Theodore Drier, close friends, and a few other Germans joined the Germans in

Tsingtau to fight for Germany. And then, after a few weeks Japan declares war on Germany. Germany never expected it

In Tsingtau, Otto was in bed with dysentery. They had a corporal, and the corporal made the people get up very early in the morning to maneuver. And there were a number of soldiers who had dysentery. It is a disease in the Orient that almost everybody gets. And he made those sick people get up and start to maneuver in their dysentery. Otto couldn't go, he was very sick, and he went into the toilet and while he was in the toilet a bullet went right through his bed. He came back and there was a bullet in the wall. If he'd been in bed he would have been killed.

The war lasted six weeks, from August to October, 1914, and then they had to surrender. And all the soldiers were taken as prisoners to Japan and they were sitting there from 1914 to 1920. Otto was also taken prisoner; he was the only one who knew how to escape. Well, he was very much liked by the Chinese, and they helped him.

Just before the Japanese entered Tsingtau, Otto crawled during the night into the office and tore out the last sheet of the lists. There was a book with all the names of the soldiers that were there, and Otto with Wiesinger was on the last page. He had been in the war there and knew where everything was and at night he sneaked into the office. He knew where it was, nothing was locked there, and he tore out that page so they didn't have his name. When the Japanese inquired about him, he said he was not with the army but a tourist caught in the net of affairs. Since they did not find his name in the list, they let him roam. So he roamed himself out of the camp, the only one amongst all the personnel.

Otto Wiesinger in Tsingtau, 1914

(Otto is the soldier without the gun belt)

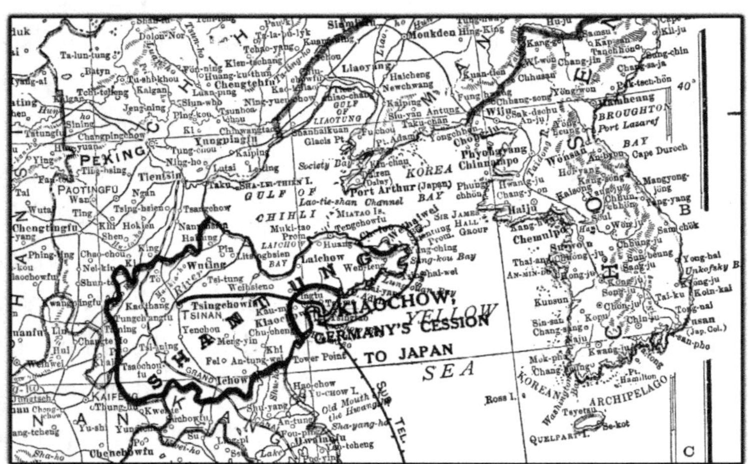

Tsingtau, Shantung Peninsula
German Colony

The way he did it, he sneaked out of the encampment during the night and in the morning boarded a Chinese coal truck that was going to the city. He was on the truck and was asked by the guards who he was and where he was going. He answered that he wanted to go into the city, but the guard refused to let him in. And that's just what he wanted. He waited for the truck to go in, unload and return and then joined the driver and drove away. At that time the Chinese were very friendly to the Germans.

He then hid in a Chinese village outside of Tsingtau until he was well enough to continue inland. This travel by foot and rickshaw and wheelbarrow and foot again compared almost with Gulliver's travels. He always went on with the assistance of the Chinese from village to village until he reached Shanghai. The Chinese had not entered the war then.

He walked. The Chinese helped him, and he walked for eight days, from Tsingtau on the Peninsula all the way to Shanghai. And everywhere the Chinese helped him, the Chinese knew the stories, they didn't like the Japanese and they hated to have them come and take over. Then, he left his money in the German bank, stored 25 barrels of German dyes with all the stock he had and boarded an American ship for the United States.

If the Kaiser had had any brains, he would have given the Shantung Peninsula back to the Chinese. That would have saved 5,000 men. He never got them back anyhow until after the war (WWI). Because the Germans didn't give the Shantung Peninsula back to the Chinese, and the Japanese went in there, the Chinese hated the Japanese and they hated the Germans. And the 5,000 German prisoners were sitting in Japan from 1914 to 1920.

As long as China was not at war, the foreigners could move freely as they liked, but as soon as China entered the war, the British lined up the Germans and the Austrians and like cattle placed them on freighters without doctors or nurses and, I believe, sent them to Australian concentration camps. The Japanese took the Germans from Tsingtau to Japan where they were for five years in concentration camps. The Chinese, watching what was going on amongst the whites, lost all respect for them; never had the white man regained the prestige he had before the war. The British and the French had acted abominably toward the white race, and I believe that they are still paying for it.

Of course, it was was the Kaiser's greatest stupidity to ask the small garrison at Tsingtau even to start a defense, since they could not replace men nor ammunition, while they were facing forty million Japanese. But what would not stupid people do for Kaiser and Vaterland? Of course, they were so sure to win, the thought of defeat never entered the picture. Otto wrote a book about Tsingtau:

> ***Als Kriegstreiwilliger in Tsingtau. Bilder und Erlebnisse aus der Belagerungszeit.*** Shanghai. 1915. Verlag von Max Nossier & Co.,E.m.b.h. Shanghai. *(**As Volunteer in Tsingtau. Pictures and Experiences of the War**)*
> Now at the Hoover Institution, Stanford

CHAPTER FIVE
World War I

When a man was engaged to go out to the Orient with a firm, he was generally engaged for three years. After three years he got a vacation of three months and the firm paid for his trip to Europe to go home for his vacation. So in 1913 Otto had his first vacation. He came to New York and from New York went home to Germany. He visited me in New York and he stayed for about a week; he went via America to go back to Hamburg and then back to Germany.

After we met in New York for a few days and he went on to the boat, I accompanied him and, as usual for Otto, we were late arriving and the boat almost left without him. I had on a toque hat. In those days it was not usual for a gentleman to kiss a lady to whom he was not engaged openly on the street. I was real shocked when he grabbed me in front of everybody and smacked me. I was so surprised that my hat flew off right into the Atlantic ocean, which was between the pier and the boat. Howling laughter from everywhere followed, but the horn blew and Otto disappeared. All I could do was wave to him.

When Otto came in 1915 to America on an American boat he had a magazine full of German dyes and indigo. If he had brought it to America, he would have become a millionaire, because when the war broke out they had no German dyes here. They dyed the flags with American dyes and all the flags lost their colors. Then, China declared war on Germany and confiscated all of his dyes. Funny how things happen; everybody thought the war would last six weeks or two or three months and end. Nobody dreamt that it would last four years.

Westliche Post, Freitag, den 10. Dezember 1915.

Zukunft von Tsingtau.

Otto Wießinger, ein Geschäftsmann aus Shanghai, gibt seine Ansicht kund.

Deutschland wird mit Japan sehr bald einig werden

Zagheit der Engländer gefällt Bundesgenossen nicht.

Westiche Post, Dec. 10, 1915.
Otto speaks in Chicago and
Milwaukee on the war in
Tsingtau, China.

By the time he arrived here the Chinese government under great pressure from the Allies declared war on Germany, so Otto lost all his fortune in Shanghai. It was simply confiscated; if he had only brought the dyes with him he could have made a fortune. There was a terrible shortage here of German dyes, and prices jumped fantastically.

Otto and Ethel Marry

Well, Otto arrived in 1915 and stayed in Chicago. In Chicago he lectured for the German Red Cross, lectured for German societies to collect money for Germany. There was a very anti-German feeling in this country already. The French and the English did a terrific propaganda job; still, it did not reach its height until the sinking of the Lusitania *(May 7, 1915.)* The climax came with the sinking of the ship, and from then on all things German were abolished, the propaganda grew sky high. While some things might have been true, the fiction was unbelievable. Many stories that were read during the war were officially denied after the war. Whatever it may be, they sure made up for it and saw to it that it was true before and after the Second World War.

I was accepted at college but I didn't go because Otto came back and then I got busy with Otto. And we walked together and associated for three years, from 1914 to 1916. In 1916 Romania entered the war. He always hoped that the war would be overnight, that the war would only last a few weeks, and then only a few months. And then when it lasted one year and it lasted a second year he ran out of money. He telegraphed to his father and his father sent him $25,000. And so he stayed another year, thinking the war would be over.

Ethel Liebman Wiesinger
New York, 1916

Then Romania entered the war. He said "Well it's no use waiting, we don't know, let's get married." So on Saturday, we went to Hoboken and we got married. We rented an apartment on Riverside Drive in New York, and I telephoned to my parents that I was married and I'm in that apartment. That almost killed the poor people. But eventually they had to recuperate and that was it. But my entire family, my father's sister, and her children, ostracized me. They gave me up. They wouldn't associate with me anymore. I didn't give a damn. I didn't like them anyway.

I married when I was 26; I never worked. I went to school I had to go a year to school in New York in order to enter college. Then Otto came in 1915 to New York. He said nothing doing about college.

We got married in 1916. I was married on the second of September and Christmas came along. And we lived in New York on 75th street, and Otto said he's going to buy me a fur jacket. That was the most important thing in my life, because a Hudson seal fur jacket was the style. When I was not married I would not have thought about buying myself a Hudson seal coat but as a married Mrs. Wiesinger; we went to Kaufman, the biggest furrier on Fifth Avenue in New York and be bought for me what I thought at that time was the most beautiful finger-tip length Hudson seal coat. That was the height of my life. I put it on and immediately went down to my parents on who lived in Brooklyn. And I have a few cousins and I knew they would be jealous if they saw my coat. I was 26 years old.

It was a wonderful time, I was in love, I was married to a wonderful man and he died a wonderful man.

Otto Karl Georg Christof Wiesinger
New York, 1916

We associated only with German people. In the German club, the German ambassador from Bürgenstock *(Switzerland)* used to come to the German club, and all the opera stars. The Germans, they were all sent back to Germany, they lost their jobs. It was a terrific time. You know, a lot of the propaganda that was told here was not true.

Once, the *Vaterland,* the most beautiful ship that Germany built, the biggest ship, the *Vaterland* was in New York. And it was a big Christmas party. And we were invited to celebrate the Christmas party on the *Vaterland.* And I wanted to wear a certain dress. And Otto didn't want me to wear that dress, I don't know why. and we didn't go to the party, we had a terrible battle. "If I can't wear that dress I'm not going," and we didn't. And it was the last party on the *Vaterland* because then the war broke out, and America took the *Vaterland* over and called it the *Leviathan,* changed the name to *Leviathan.* But that time I could've died because I couldn't wear that dress.

Thinking back now I realize it was difficult when we were first married, Otto and I; I mean economically because Otto couldn't get a job. He was German, blacklisted. A very big chemical house in the states that still exists, Johnson and Johnson, Otto went to them and they took him right away, gave him a job. He was an educated man; he wasn't an everyday person. But the people in the office were so mean to him he had to leave, he couldn't hold a job. One time he came in and there was a big blood red hand on his desk because the propaganda against Germany was so terrible during the war, First World War. This was at a very big factory, the biggest chemical in this country.

And then we couldn't go everywhere. In New York, we could only go a certain circle around because he was blacklisted. It was when we were first married.

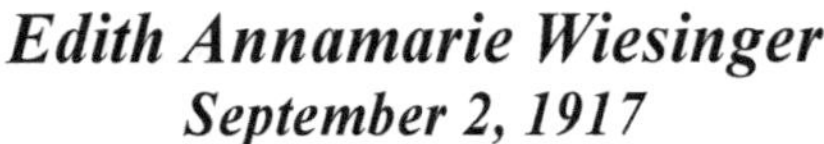

Edith Annamarie Wiesinger
September 2, 1917

New York

I was very happy with him, I was very much in love, and within a year, on my wedding day I got Edith. I was married in 1916 and she was born in 1917, the second of September. I was young and happy and he was a wonderful man and his father sent him 75,000 marks so we had money to live on.

Making a Living in War Time

There were a lot of Germans in New York and they had a very beautiful club. We were members of the German club. They supported the arts. When I came to New York in 1912, most of the opera stars were German and we met them all. Otto Goritz was a very good friend of ours. He was one of the most famous tenors.

The German club issued a book, a very thick book with members, and Otto went around and sold advertisements for that book. And made quite a lot of money; a lot of money he could make. And we were in a brownstone house, 47 West 90th Street, one of those brownstone houses. Then we moved out of that house to 86th Street. We were not rich but we had enough money.

Of course the minute America declared war, Otto was on the blacklist and it was tough for him to do anything. He sold advertisements for the German club magazine to make some money that way until he met a son-in-law of the Liebmann family who are brewers in New York. Otto formed a corporation with him; they owned the Liebmann Brewery. Seemingly we are not related and I don't remember how he got the connection. Anyhow, this son-in- law was a society man, but not a successful businessman; he provided the capital and Otto the know-how. This was the middle of 1917. He started as a broker, meaning he found some chemicals that others needed and some dyes, and other items that were hard to get. It was quite prosperous, and Edith was born. Then one day Otto read that Washington was very short of tungsten, a mineral needed in electrical work, light work, light bulbs and other things. Ingenious as he was, Otto knew a Chinese in Hong Kong who had mines there and who mined tungsten.

Edith Wiesinger

New York, 1919

He immediately wired to his Chinese friends and sure enough he could get the mineral. He immediately spoke to Washington, and in spite of the restrictions, he was permitted to come to Washington and received an order right there and then. He placed his order in Hong Kong, and when the first shipment arrived it earned $145,000 for his firm. Everybody was elated.

In the meantime the war and the hatred progressed. Liebmann put in another order, the government bought; then another order and then it was found out, or the partner reported it through a stooge, that Otto was a partner in the business. The firm had the alternative to either close or dissolve partnership with Otto because he was German. It was then agreed that Otto should voluntarily resign. An agreement was reached that Otto should leave and they will provide him with a monthly salary for about three months and give advice to his partner. He was assured that after the war all his shares would be delivered to him. He could not do anything to protect himself.

By that time his partner, who was always a high society man and playboy, thought he does not need Otto anymore. He could order tungsten himself. Otto strongly advised against it; unless having a written order not to touch it. But the man did not listen; Otto was overruled. The shipment was ordered and by the time it was shipped and arrived in New York rumors were already that the war will end very soon. The good luck of the office was over. Armistice was declared and tungsten sank to its lowest level, from $27 per unit to $5 per unit. The firm went bankrupt. They lost every cent they made; the office was closed. So we stood with nothing, wondering where and when our next meal will come from. We wanted to go right away to Germany but here too the blacklist was used and we had to wait two years before we could leave.

What to do now? We had rented a house at 113 W. 86 Street, a brownstone house. The basement had a kitchen and a servant's dining room; the first floor was a parlor and dining room and pantry; the second floor had two connecting bedrooms--one was Edith's; the top floor had servant quarters which we did not use. We decided to rent one floor that would help pay the rent.

We made our bedrooms on the third floor, rented our two bedrooms as living and bedroom. Well, the first answer to our ad was two very nice girls they were willing to take the rooms at $90.00 per month and I was in heaven. In the course of the conversation they said, "You understand that we are receiving guests," and I looked at them naively and said "Of course," otherwise why would they want a living room? So they moved in and everything was honey.

A few days later a neighbor came in and said, "Who are those officers who walked out at six in the morning?" "Officers?" I said "What officers?" "Well," she said, "I saw them come out of your house," I was surprised, but still did not know what it all was until Otto came home. I said to him that our neighbor told me she saw two officers leave our house early in the morning, I don't understand. Well, he said, you are too dumb, I bet they are prostitutes. Up he went confronting them with the idea. The idea, of course! They said "We receive guests, and we told your wife and she said it was all right." Well, they had to pack right there and then and leave the house, *Mein Gott, sagt papa, wie dumm kann man sein (My God, he said, how dumb can you you be?)* he was just wild at me. I never dreamed that. I was so stupid. When he got mad he had to swear in German and I got plenty of it.

We then had a nice German family from Manila who stayed with us until we gave up the house and went to Germany.

The propaganda was terrific. There was an entire movie picture, pictures taken on the German battlefields. They said such terrible stories about them.

Ethel and Edith Wiesinger
Christmas, 1922

Hamburg, Germany

CHAPTER SIX
Visiting Hamburg

We married in 1916; in 1920 we went to Germany. We couldn't get any visas sooner. Otto was in the war in Tsingtau, he was on the blacklist. We went to Germany on the beautiful Swedish boat to stay with his father. His father was still alive.

We left about the 20th of July 1920 on the Swedish steamer *Helig Olav* for Germany. Edith was three years old and was going to *Grampa Deutschland.* It was a beautiful boat and a very smooth trip, we arrived in Oslo on a wonderful morning, and the first thing we all wanted to do was to go ashore. Well, we did not figure with the red tape that ruled the world after the war; we did not think of taking out visas just for one day of call in Oslo. So there the passengers stood and looked at the skyline of Oslo, and could not set foot on the land.

But Otto was different. He thought of a way. He went to our cabin, put on his overcoat and a cap on his head, walked up on deck, passed me as if he never saw me nor the other passengers, saluted the policeman, who stood at the bridge taking good care that nobody walks off, and left the boat. The policeman thought he was one of the officials. He returned to the boat before it was ready to leave in the evening, and nobody had missed him or questioned him.

Then, on to Copenhagen where we stayed three days at the Palace Hotel. Edith was three years old and cute as could be. Edith and I took a tour of the city, and above all she wanted to see the Rosenborg Castle, and all she talked about was the castle, until we arrived there.

Walter Wiesinger
Otto's Brother

Author
Die Entwicklung des Notenbankenwesens in den Vereinigten Staaten von Amerika unter besonderer Berücksichtigung des Aldrich-Planes und des Federal-Reserve-Acte vom 23. Dezember 1913] *Publisher: Jena [1921*

(The development of central banking in the United States, with special reference to the Aldrich Plan and the Federal Reserve Act of December 23, 1913)

She was fast asleep and awoke when we had to leave the bus after arriving back at our hotel. While having dinner at the dining room, she roamed around and finally stopped in front of the three-man band. We watched her talking. She walked over to the violinist, watched him fiddle a long time. When she finally returned to our table we asked what you said to the man, and she answered, the man said he wants a piece of bread and butter and I said he can't have any. I will never know how she conversed in English and he in Danish.

Otto's Family

From Copenhagen we went to Hamburg where Grandfather awaited us. His wife had passed away in 1915; he kept a *hausdame (housekeeper)* Fräulein Schreiber, and Anna the cook. He was a very lonesome man, had retired from his office but due to the war he had been called back since he was the only authority on taxes and customs.

Arriving about ten o'clock PM, Grandfather was there waiting for us, and Edith took to him immediately. He was Grampa Deutschland *(Grampa Germany),* while my father was Grampa Brooklyn. Grampa Deutschland was 74 years old. He is, up to today, quoted as the authority in the German Meyers Encyclopedia. Otto was very fond and proud of his father.

Otto was the successful son while Walter went along in Berlin, from job to job. However after the war Walter went back to the university made his doctor of something with summa cum laude, and became a director of the Berlin Royal Library.

We drove to Grampa's residence which was an apartment in a four-apartment building. Arriving, we entered a large square entrance hall that led into a large *herrenzimmer,* the library, then a large *damensalon, (women's parlor)* then a large general salon, then a large dining room and finally a guest room that was ours. The first thing I saw was that the beds were a mile apart. We immediately got busy and pushed them together.

Edith made a big hit with grandpa, and he called the pastor, I think he was the Jacobean who had confirmed Otto, to baptize her. It was quite an affair. I held one of Edith's hands and Otto the other; she stood still watching what was going on. But when the minister started to pour a handful of water over her, she just ran away, so that she received the Father, the Son, but not the Holy Spirit.

The following week I left for Vienna and Otto for Switzerland. When I returned after three weeks Edith opened the door for me, Anna behind her, and spoke German. In November Otto returned to New York.

I remained with Otto's father; shortly afterwards he became sick. On the lower floor a Doctor Kluege lived and he took care of Grampa. There was nothing one could do, he had cancer of the bladder and died the 10th of January. He was buried on Otto's birthday the 14th. He was a very fine man. At the funeral there all the big shots of the town and Otto's brother Walter came from Berlin. Then I had to receive the condolences, and keep the household going until, I was told by the authorities, that I have no right to the quarters, that I was not a citizen and therefore will have to vacate. I held an auction, sold most of the furnishings except the things that Otto's brother chose to keep, and then I left for Passau where I stayed with Aunt Marie, Otto's real mother's sister, as a paying house guest until fall. Then I traveled back to Hamburg boarded the SS Cleveland and returned to New York.

Business Troubles

All in all, we stayed a year in Germany and stayed with family. Before leaving, Otto opened an office in Hamburg; I stayed in Germany with his father while he went to China and opened an office in China. He had an office in New York. So we had three offices, one in New York, one in Hamburg and one in Shanghai. Then I joined him in China in 1924.

Otto left for Shanghai; he opened an office there with a guy who had no experience at all, and so the two, the office in Hamburg and the one in Shanghai, brought us to the verge of bankruptcy.

One day Otto received a telegram from the guy in Shanghai: remit ten thousand dollar otherwise will have to close the office. I had a party that evening, and did not know about the telegram. Otto was very quiet that evening, but after everybody left, he let loose. "Where can I get ten thousand dollars," he asked me: "Well," I said "do you have any intention of sending that guy money?" "I cannot let that office close. I have to send the money." Fortunately he could not get the money and so he was forced to close the office.

Then came Hamburg. Things were going from bad to worse. So one day Otto comes home, pulls a steamship ticket from his pocket and says "I cannot leave for Hamburg, I have an important lawsuit pending here, so you pack and go." It was a Saturday; Wednesday I was on the boat.

Otto had the idea to open an office in Hamburg in 1920. He had had an agent there before. So instead of getting an agent, he employed a young man who was the brother of a man that had worked with him in New York. Reinike was a very nice young man and Otto had an office in New York and Reinike worked with Otto. And so when Otto was in Hamburg and he corresponded with Reinike about imports from Germany to America, and to China, and from America to Germany, he told him he wanted to open an office in Hamburg.

CHARTERED EXPORT & IMPORT CORPORATION, 46 Vesey Street, New York. Established 1919. Telephone: Cortlandt 1721. Cable address: "Atpatraco, New York." Codes: A B C 5th Improved, Lieber's, Bentley's. New York Corporation. President. Otto Wiesinger; Vice President and Treasurer, Walter Reinicke; Secretary, Paul Schaaphaus. Operated by Excelsior Dyestuff & Chemical Co.
Own House: Shanghai.
Agencies: Hamburg, Danzig, Crefeld, Copenhagen, Stockholm.
Other Foreign Markets: Japan.
Exports: Chemicals, dyestuffs, oils, cotton, wool, linters, soap, Turkey red oil, general merchandise.
Imports: Chemicals, dyes, colors, artificial silk, embroideries, laces, hair nets, general merchandise.

And Reinike writes back to Otto in Hamburg that my brother is in Hamburg and he has been a businessman and if you open an office, why don't you take him, Herbert Reinike, to manage your office in Hamburg? And Otto, very naive not making any inquiries: if it's Reinike's brother, there's no necessity to inquire about him, who he was, what he was. Because Reinike was a very fine young man so his brother must also be a fine young man. So Reinike is in Hamburg, Otto rents and office and fixes it up and puts him in as manager of the office.

And that is one of the worst things he did because Reinike was no good. It cost us an awful lot of money, and finally Otto comes home and says "Ethel, I've bought a ticket on a Norwegian boat. You are leaving Sunday for Hamburg." On the boat, I had a platonic love affair with a priest, all the way from New York to Hamburg; why he was a priest I'll never know. It was a very lovely trip and I arrive in Hamburg. I was supposed to find out what was going on in Otto's office where Reinike was the manager.

When I arrived in Hamburg Mr. Reinicke said I have no authority and have no right even to come to the office, he refused to give me any information. I come to Hamburg to that office and I'm treated like a piece of stone. They wouldn't even give me a smile. I asked "Where are the books?" He said, "I have the books at home. I do my book keeping at home."

I was sitting there quite a few weeks and I wrote back to Otto that I can't find out a thing, and that irked me. I found out from a girl there that he had a bookkeeper, that Reinike had a bookkeeper, and that the books were not at Reinike's home. The bookkeeper took the books home, so there was nothing I could look up in the office to find out what they were doing. But we had to pay the rent for the office, and he had a secretary and we had to pay the salary; Otto sent the money from New York to keep the office open. There was no business.

Otto finally decided to join me in Hamburg. His partner must have notified his brother, because as Otto's boat entered Hamburg harbor, another boat left carrying Reinicke his wife and son to New York. The ships crossed each other. We found an empty office bare of everything including all the books.

Reinicke's bookkeeper had worked in cahoots with him and lived with his mother in a suburb of Hamburg. When Otto contacted the bookkeeper and asked for information he laughed in his face and said "I don't have to give you any information, I was not in your employee but Mr. Reinicke's. Where are the books? I don't know."

Then I came with an idea, if this man lives with his mother, then, since he had no job anymore, maybe I can innocently contact her, inquire whether her son is available for another position, and see how far I can go to find out about Reinicke and the books. It was easy to find the address, and there I went. I dressed myself up very nice and during the day

I walked over to that mother. The old lady was alone, I came in and inquired about her son, of course he was not there.

"Too bad," I said I need him very badly. "I have a job for him that nobody else could do. I heard he was very smart and could help me." "What kind of a job is it?" "Well," I said, "I am a widow and have a business and I think that my manager is robbing me, I would like your son to go over the books without these people knowing it, but how could we do it?" "Oh," she said "that's funny, my son just had such a job, and he managed to get the books out, and they are right here, I am sure be can help you." "Good," I said, "I will call him up and see what he can do for me."

I left and within half an hour I was home, Otto got the police, went to the house and the books were confiscated. Then we saw that he did business with Russia and that he worked for himself, not for Otto who paid the bills. Thousands of dollars. There was a stack of telegrams that he was telegraphing between him and either Finland or Russia with merchandise, a stack that thick. That was the end of the Hamburg office.

I wonder what that poor women got from her raving son. But what good was it? Otto sued the absent Reinecke, won a reparation suit, which did him no good since Reinecke was in the states and if he ever returned to Germany, Otto was not there to catch him. That was another episode in Otto's life.

CHAPTER SEVEN
China in the 1920's

I arrived in Shanghai on my birthday in 1924 *(March23)* and stayed until December 1926. I liked people, and by entertaining I felt I was very important. I always entertained an awful lot and nobody ever refused when I invited them. My table was always set for one more than we invited, and there was always one more. I had a different education, a broader education and I was very well read. They always asked me what to read. I was very well informed about writers and musicians and artists and I was interested in the intellectual world. And there were always interesting leading conversations when they came to my house, there was always life in my house. Men were interested in talking to me. The women were like here, they talked about other things than the intellectual.

We associated only with German people. I did not know that one of the very well-known women, her husband was a big businessman there, I didn't know that she was an alcoholic. I found it out later. I always wondered why she clung to me. And she flattered me, and I didn't know why. It is difficult to recognize these things. I'd never dealt with alcoholic affairs. Otto was not an alcoholic; he had two highballs and got a little sleepy.

In China, you never invited a man alone, unless he came with his wife. There was one woman who was very intellectual who spoke a perfect French and English, Mrs. Teifenbacher. German women from Germany, only educated women came out. The German men came to

Otto, Ethel and Edith

Shanghai, China
1925

China single and then they went home and got married; they always married girls from fine, educated cultural families. If they brought a girl out of the lower classes, she wouldn't have been accepted.

At the parties they would play the piano and would sing; they would be familiar with all the classics. We were all on the same level, as far as schoolwork was concerned. Intellectually, you still have your own intellect; how you use your education and if you use it at all. I'm sure there were women there who never even spoke of Goethe or Schiller or Grillparzer or Lessing or any of those, but they knew of them, they had to study them in school. They were women of the better classes. The men couldn't bring home just a nobody. I could always hold a conversation with men. I was always interested in the latest books and the latest writers and the latest plays and the latest theater and opera. And then mahjong came out. And did we play mahjong.

I used to dress in the afternoon and go downtown, drive down in the ritzy downtown to the Palace Hotel and the managers of the big firms with their wives, and they have tea around five o'clock.

I'll never forget one time. We were having tea at the Palace Hotel in Shanghai, all the heads of the biggest concerns were sitting at the tables, and they had such ignorance of what was going on in China. One of them said I don't know what is happening here, whether China is going to pieces or whether China is going to be reborn or something will happen. Something is going on. They didn't know that communists were working very hard and the Chinese were fighting among themselves at that time. The communists and the

Ethel Wiesinger, 1925

Shanghai, China
(Newly Bobbed Hair)

non-communists, they were not working in international circles with white people, nobody knew. They never realized what was going on in China. The Chinese wealthier people, the business people, did not know what was going on among the coolies. The coolies began to wake up to communism. So it was a terrible time for all of them.

Every afternoon I used to go downtown, and sometimes I'd take Edith along and go to the Palace Hotel, the first class hotel in Shanghai. We'd meet there at a table for tea at five o'clock in the evening, all the bosses of the big firms, and we'd sit all together with their wives or alone and we would have five o'clock tea. And after tea at 5:30, 6:00 the men would go back to their offices. I'd go home and they would come home at 7:00. 7:30. And at 8:30 we'd have dinner, and we'd always set the table.

The English were very stuffy. They had a club of 99 people. You had to have horns to be admitted to that club. And finally they were kicked out of China the same as the Germans, but before then they made a terrible mistake, the British. They arrested all the Germans in Shanghai and drove them like coolies to cheap freight boats. 1914. The British lined up the Germans and the Austrians and like cattle placed them on freighters without doctors or nurses and, I believe, sent them to Australian concentration camps.

So the Chinese, watching what was going on amongst the whites, lost the respect that they had for white people, for to them, they were only white people, whether they were British or German or French, no difference.

And they were only Chinese to us; they had differences the way we have differences. They speak different Chinese in different colonies. They don't understand each other. If I had a servant who came from Shantung and a servant who

Otto Wiesinger, 1925

Shanghai, China

Map of Shanghai, 1910

came from Ningpo they couldn't talk to each other. But we didn't know that.

Nobody went in to study. There were a few students but they didn't amount to anything.

There was a distinct difference where the Chinese lived and where the Europeans lived. We lived in the international circle where there was a French community and a British community, and between the two, the others, the non-British and non-French lived. We lived in French town, on Bubbling Well Road. We had a lovely house there. *(It was in the French Quarter; Edith went to first, second and third grade in the German school. When Edith visited China years later, their apartment was then part of the Russian Embassy building.)*

Otto spoke Cantonese Chinese. It's a little easier to understand. I don't know how he learned it or how much he knew but he could converse with Chinese. How limited it was I can't tell. There is no grammar; there is no alphabet. You have to remember each word. If you don't know it you just don't know it. You know: I came, I am coming, I will come, no such thing. They are all different words that he had to study each word. He knew one man, a Mr. Kan, a stock broker, he was supposed to know ten thousand Chinese words, and he was the only one like that we knew.

I didn't learn much from the Chinese people. I had no time. I was too busy entertaining and having a good time. When I managed my servants and took care of Edith and took care of the two Japanese maids, one for Edith and one for me, and took care of tennis and took care of entertaining, that's all we could do is entertain. I had nothing to do with the Chinese except with the servants, and I had to go to the store to shop. It was a very peculiar life. I attempted to study Chinese for six months and I gave up. It was too difficult. I couldn't do it. I took it from a Chinese girl; she was half Chinese, half Chinese and half European. I don't know who her father was. Her mother was Chinese. She spoke English very well.

We had a houseboy by the name of Chu, he was very tall and came from Ningpo. Ningpo is a town in the interior and every Chinaman who landed in Shanghai came from "Ningpo more far," just like every Austrian comes from Vienna. Also when they suddenly disappeared and you asked where is so and so, the answer was always "Ningpo more far." Chu could not talk pidgin English nor any other language that a foreigner could understand. Therefore I was the interpreter because we really did not know where he came from and he could not understand the other servants in the house. However, he learned very fast and in a few months he could take the place of the number one boy, or the amah, even the cook. When we bought the first car that was a Chandler, and the chauffeur had suddenly gone to Ningpo more far, Otto came downstairs found the car in front of the house. He asked, "Who took the car out?" Of course it was Chu who had somehow learned to drive.

When Father received a shipment of bicycles from England and some of them arrived broken, he asked Chu to come to the warehouse and clean them up. Not only did he clean them but also repaired every one and learned in no time how to ride them.

Once I had a fight with him and discharged him. He was away three weeks. He was sick about it and so was I. He had taken a job with Czechoslovaks and could not understand them so he came back and asked for his job and I took him back for a dollar less than I had paid him before. Father was crazy about Chu and we surely would have brought him to the United States but at that time our own circumstances were insecure and the difficulties in getting an immigration permit very great so we had to leave him there. He sure was a jewel and a genius. Goodness knows what he would have become if he had a chance.

As long as China was not at war, the foreigners could move freely as they liked. It was such an incredible life, how the white people lived in the Orient, in India, in China; not so in Japan. In Japan we were already more restricted. The Japanese did not let the white person walk on them like the Chinese did. When I came to America you had to go via Japan, so I stayed two, three days with some friends in Japan.

Doing Business In Shanghai

There was something about the Chinese that appealed to Otto. He never made a contract with a Chinaman. Whatever he sold to them, they came in and give an order, and when the order arrived, they would accept it and they would pay it and that was it. There were other things that appealed to him. He was very fond of the Chinese.

They never made a contract. When they gave Otto a contract for thousands and thousands of dollars, they used a comprador as a buyer, a Chinese comprador. Depending on the size of the business, the comprador was important; a big firm would have a big comprador with background, the customer would come to the comprador and say give me 10,000 lamps. They used oil. No contract was signed. The comprador would come to Otto and say this man wants 10,000 Irish lamps. Otto would go to the big English bank and open a letter of credit. He would put out the order, the loans would come in, the Chinaman would pay, they would go to the bank and pay off the loans, and he would take the profit and it was settled. Not a word was written down.

When artificial silk came out *(rayon),* there was a great demand for it. It was cheap, it was washable, and the first big business was down in Italy. Italian people had big factories of artificial silk, and of course, Otto had an agent in Hamburg who was always looking for new merchandise to send out to Otto, samples, that he could sell to the Chinese. So he sent some samples of silk and Otto had bought quite a number of it, I don't know why, exactly, he gave a big order for silk and the order arrived too late, and the people refused to accept it. .

And there was no such thing as you could sell it to somebody else in China; if the people who gave you the order did not accept the merchandise you could just as well throw the merchandise out. Otto ordered the artificial silk from Italy and in that you generally say it has to arrive within 90 days or 30 days. You never imported anything unless you had a contract.

Otto was supposed to bring in some weapons to fight communism, to fight the war against communism, 1924-25. On the first of January, on Sylvester Eve *(New Year's Eve),* I gave a big party and the telephone came that the ship arrived and you must come immediately. So we left the party and he took a boat and I think he went to Chungking where the ammunition was supposed to be delivered. When he arrived it was cold and icy and they had to take it off to deliver it, but it was never delivered to the people who bought it. The communists took it over. Otto safely came home; it was a miracle.

Later the Chinese leader in North China, Chang Tso-lin, was murdered. From that time on, the anti-communists lost all power. They couldn't fight it any more. That's when Mao Tse Tung started the way up to the north his communism. It's a very famous incident in the communist life. So Otto came back and then we decided it is no use, Otto had a building, a square block and the second floor was vacant; he did all his business on the first floor of the building, Number 6 Kiangsi Road. *(Chang Tso-lin, that is, Zhang, Zuolin (1875–1928) was the warlord of Manchuria from 1916 to 1928, He was defeated by Chiang Kai-shek in May 1928. and killed; his brief reign foreshadowed the end of Chinese war lords.)*

The white colonists, British and French and German, they did not know what was going on in China. They still thought they could keep China a colony country. England had practically the entire coast of China, they took Hong Kong, they had all the coast up, and the French had a colony there, Germany had Tsingtau, a big peninsula and they all thought they could remain and be the big shots. And they didn't see what was going on in China. They never took the trouble to read the Chinese paper, I assume.

Otto spoke Cantonese and they loved him. They just loved him, and he did a terrific business. Very few of the Europeans spoke Chinese, very, very few. I spoke German and English. I had English in school in Europe, and French. I had my English and my French in Austria.

One time there was a terrific battle in Chinatown. Otto had a big square building, his offices, and the second floor was empty. It was a big building, a corner building, and all the offices on the corner had about 20 or 30 people working, Chinamen, working for him. And the upper floor was empty. Otto permitted his employees to bring their families to live on the second floor, and they stayed there for a month or six weeks because the communists had gotten into Chinatown in Shanghai and were fighting the non-communists. There was a terrific battle, a terrific war. And it was already a war between communists and non-communist. I can't say anti-communists because I didn't know whether they were for or against. They didn't know what communism was.

And at that time it was already going on big in China and the white people didn't know a thing about it. Until one day, they came into Otto's office, a group of communists, and they started to destroy the tables and chairs and bookcases, they threw them over. 1926. And then they began to inquire what was going on and they saw what was coming.

It wasn't easy for China to become a communist country. I think it was very good for China because the difference from person to person was indescribable. There was no charity; there were no doctors except the Chinese doctors who had acupuncture. There were no hospitals to go to. You could sell your children like you sold a chicken. I think only communism was the means by which they could eventually wake up to a 20th century way of life.

Now, of course they have a billion people, I don't know how they live there now, but at the time that I was living there they had the rickshaws and the rickshaw coolies; they used to pay beggars and cripple them purposely to lay them on the streets where the people who passed by would throw them a few pennies. There was no mercy; charity was unknown. So I think communism was a wonderful thing for the Chinese, to wake them up that there are other ways of life than what they thought was the proper way of life.

Shipping Arms To China

When the revolution in China started in 1910, the greatest part of the Chinese population did not know what was going on; the great changes took place in Peking and the few larger cities around the country. Here the various so-called generals learned and practiced the fortunes of war. When they were sent out to govern the various provinces, they exploited the population by levying taxes for the following ten years, collecting it in advance and then they fled. Small generals made wars on each other, and the poor population was between pillar and post, with no hope of ever having peace. Their stores were looted, their crops confiscated by greedy generals, This went on for years, until they lost all interest to work the fields, Starvation and sickness was all over the country.

During that time there was one great politician and general in Mongolia, his name I believe was Chang Tso-lin. He was a great warlord, and had many friends in Shanghai and Hong Kong who financed him. It seemed they hoped that if he could defeat the many small looting generals, he could become the sole ruler of China. At that time Germany was in high esteem by the Chinese. Otto was a prominent member of the German group in Shanghai and so in 1925 he was approached with an offer to buy and supply them with war material.

Germany had a law at the time that prohibited the export of weapons to China. Well, after a lot of negotiations between the Chinese and Otto, he got an order for one half million pounds sterling. There were to be only guns and ammunition, no machine guns or larger weapons. Through an agent in Germany the guns were bought and shipped to Italy. There a German steamer, the *Nordmark*, was chartered. The crew was German and had a contract to take the ship to China and then they were to be shipped back to where they were hired. The captain was an old seahorse. So everything was set. Well, Otto's profit on the deal was 100.000 dollars, Chinese dollars. He was just forty years old. Everything went along well. And the warlords sat on their hands waiting for the shipment of arms to arrive. In the meantime, the enemies have also ordered war materials, and it was a question as to who will get it first.

The *Nordmark* was to go straight through the Suez Canal to China. Here is where the tragedy begins. The captain, instead of following orders, decided to go to Durban, Africa, for some unexplained reason. He said that a sailor had an injured arm and he was afraid that blood poisoning would set in. The sailors said that it was not so, though he had an injured arm, it was not that bad. Other sailors said that the captain had a sweetheart in Italy, and he expected mail. Anyhow, whatever his reason was, we could never find out. It cost us the war.

In Durban the British inspectors came on board, although they had no right to do so, examined the cargo and of all things found at the bottom of the shipment a machine gun. They made the captain unload the ship, and wanted to confiscate the cargo. Of course, they had no right to do either, and so a battle of lawyers started that cost a small fortune, and after six weeks the ship and cargo was released. To all this the British had absolutely no legal right, but who could fight the British? They took many liberties, all over the globe, and nobody could do anything about it.

The ship, having been in harbor for six weeks, collected barnacles at the bottom and that slowed down the mileage. Otto received a telegram that unless the bottom of the ship is scraped they cannot continue sailing. Also, the sailors are in mutiny because they were supposed to be home long ago. So it was decided that the ship should anchor in Batavia. But what mutiny?

Otto could not go to Batavia, because the Chinese not only became impatient but also suspicious. So they would not let Otto leave Shanghai. There was no alternative but that I should go. Edith stayed with friends. And so I went. I boarded the French steamer *Andrea Kleber* and sailed for Hong Kong, Saigon and then Singapore. There I had to take the Dutch steamer Princess Juliana and arrived in Batavia *(Indonesia)*.

I registered at the Netherland Hotel and started to wait. I must have waited two or three weeks, I only know that I was there for St. Nicholas Day, which is the Dutch Christmas in Batavia. Finally I received word from the German consulate that the *Nordmark* had arrived. The harbor is Tanjung Priok and about two hours out of Batavia. I took a taxi and drove to the harbor. There I heard from all the sailors nothing but complaints. One sailor was a communist and he said, and he was right, that they were hired for a certain length of time to go and to come back. But being four weeks in Africa, and then the ship was full of barnacles and had to be fixed, made it almost double the time that they contracted for. But the ship could not be left without sailors, and they couldn't get any sailors in Java to take the ship back to Germany or to take it up to China. The particular sailor, a communist, was dressing and intending to drive to the German consulate to place a complaint and demand to be returned immediately to Germany, not only he but the entire crew.

The harbor in Java is two hours distant from the city so you have to take a bus from the harbor to the city or from the city to the harbor. When the *Nordmark* arrived, I took a taxi; I didn't wait for a bus to take me there. And I met the captain and the captain told me of all the trouble he has on account of that sailor who was causing all that turmoil.

The German consul was on vacation, but the vice-consul was there, a handsome young man, the son of Count Zeppelin who brought in the very first airplane to America from Germany. The sailor waited for the bus to take him to the German consul to put down his complaint. Well, I had a better chance with that Count Zeppelin than he had with his bus, because when he arrived, I had told the consul the story of the ship and that the ship has to go to China. That it was German merchandise, it was a German boat, it has to go to deliver the goods and it has to go back. And I was very well dressed.

I was young and pretty and I had a wonderful time with that Count Zeppelin. I was invited to the dinner by the governor of the island of Java when the first Dutch airplane fleet came from Holland to Java. There was a big palace where the governor lived and the governor gave a big dinner party, it was unbelievable and I was invited. We were all standing on the patio and the aeroplanes were coming in, and we danced and we chatted, it was reckless. He served a gorgeous dinner in his villa and then I went home back to the hotel.

By the time that sailor arrived the consul told him if he doesn't go back and obey the orders that the captain is giving and does what he has to do, he's going to arrest him and send him back. The boat went into dock, where it took eight days to clean it, put in fresh provisions and make it ready to leave. The crew was still obstinate and refused to obey the captain. It was questionable whether it would leave at all. The pilot was waiting for the boat to be escorted out of the harbor. Well, what to do?

I got the idea of sending two large cases of beer to the ship. All knew that the ship had to leave the next day so I went out and bought twelve large cases of beer, bottle beer, and I sent it to the ship. And I told the boatswain, the boatswain is the head of the sailors, and I told him not to touch that beer until they are on the high seas, and they did not obey me. The minute the beer came on the ship they opened the cases and they all got drunk. That was not my order, but I didn't care.

At four o'clock in the morning the pilot called for me and I went with him and we went to the boat—the boatswain and the captain steered the ship out of the harbor out and when the sailors woke up they were already on the high seas. I got the beer just as a gift to appease them and to make them enjoy a bottle of beer. I really had no idea that they were going to open it right away, and get drunk. It was not my intent. But the boatswain let them open the twelve cases, huge cases. I was with the pilot in his boat, and when it was good and out, we sailed back and when the sailors awoke they were on the high seas. It was in Chungking that the ship finally docked.

I sat in the dining room of the Netherland Hotel when a bunch of newsmen arrived and they talked to the people there telling them that a German ship came in last night asking for provisions and water and coal, but was refused, and they had to leave this morning without anything. They never knew that I guided the ship out of the harbor. The next day was a big article in the newspaper repeating the story. That was the first time that I realized how the papers work.

I boarded a *Blue Funnel Liner* and sailed for home. I had a big party on New Year's Eve when a telegram arrived that father should leave at once for a northern city, the *Nordmark* had arrived and they cannot dock. An enemy boat had met the *Nordmark* and demanded the cargo. Otto left immediately. He returned from that last trip, glad to be alive. He could have easily been killed.

I don't remember how Otto met the *Nordmark*. The sea was almost frozen. He climbed the boat, convinced the strange boat to leave and nearly drowned. Then they proceeded to dock, and unload. It was exactly three months too late and therefore we lost the war. The enemy somehow had their weapons sooner.

In 1926 already, Otto was beginning to give up the business, the orders did not come in as much. Otto imported the lamps, if you read the book, *Oil for the Lamps of China. (by Hobart and Cochran, 1933; movie, 1935)* Standard Oil, they supplied the oil and Otto supplied the lamps. He imported from Ireland, thousands and thousands of oil lamps, and they banned the oil. And watches, they were crazy about watches in China. Otto had agents in Switzerland; he imported thousands of watches. But in 1926 it began to be difficult. They were hesitant in giving orders, they were hesitant to pay for them promptly as they used to. The extra cost of the shipment, the murder of Chang Tso-lin before everything was paid, left Otto without any profit. That's when Edith and I left for San Francisco.

The resistance against white people regardless of nationality grew constantly; business fell off. The Chinese word of honor, which was like the rock of Gibraltar, disappeared. Underground hate grew; then the fear of Japan, which was justified. All in all, it was very easy for the communists to enter, and we helped a lot to make it come faster. Chiang Tso-lin was murdered, and the struggle kept on all anew. The situation in China was so desperate that any one with guts could rule. Then came Chiang Kai-shek, a man not equal to the situation. He followed the old order, rather, the ancient tradition of graft, protégés; not able men but favored men were getting the good jobs. So that eventually what we have now was inevitable.

It will remain a mystery why the captain sailed to Durban, a mystery where the machine gun came from, why the British searched this particular ship, maybe the Chinese knew something about the transaction, who knows? Its all like a dream to me; I see myself on that little boat in the Java waters at the side of the pilot, and looking up at the captain at the steering wheel, it was simply beautiful.

Otto loved the Chinese and did everything he could for them but there was not much you could do. They had the impression that you must only smile when you talk to a white person, to a European person. One time a comprador came and with a smiling face he said, "My son died." They didn't expect any sympathy, it was incredible, I don't think all the books that are written about China don't mean much because they really don't know the Chinese at the time.

San Francisco, 1930

Market Street

CHAPTER EIGHT
San Francisco and the Depression Years

I arrived on the 24th of December 1926 at five o'clock in the afternoon in San Francisco, and they didn't even examine our luggage; they said, "Get Off!" because the customs officers wanted to go home for Christmas. It took me three weeks to sail to San Francisco. I came to San Francisco to my brother; I stayed three months and then went back to China leaving Edith with my brother, Ben Liebman and my sister-in-law, Jeanette. I went back to China and stayed about two months with Otto.

Otto came to San Francisco in April 1927 and said it's finished with China. But he still imported things from China because the stores were still working. He had a factory in China; he had a hair net factory. He had 300 girls making hair nets. They went out of style because people began to cut their hair. So they had to close the factory.

After arriving in San Francisco Otto went right to Gumps and Gumps gave him a big order for Chinese goods. And he went to China and I stayed with my brother with Edith. And Otto bought a big order for Gumps. *(Gumps, an elegant San Francisco store sold exotic rugs, porcelain, silks, bronzes and jade from China and Japan.)*

The Temple of Heaven

Otto thought if Gumps in San Francisco can use that merchandise – he came back and rented the store in the St. Francis Hotel. And he bought all those things, went back to China bought a terrific amount of merchandise--the duties were terrific--and he opened a store in the St. Francis Hotel.

Ethel's Brother
Jeanette, Perry and Ben Liebman

Ben Liebman left Czernowitz when he was 14 to escape conscription into the Kaiser's army. He built many houses in the Marina district of San Francisco after the earthquake of 1906; he was among the first to put garages on the ground floor. Jeanette was a milliner. His son Perry was also a builder.

The shop was called the *Temple of Heaven.* I was in business with him. I went to the store already. We were so lucky. I designed the underwear, and a nightgown, a slip, panties and a housecoat of Chinese silk all embroidered. They were just gorgeous. We sold them for $80-$90 a set. And we had a lot of Jewish and gentile and all kinds of customers would come in. All the Junior League girls; sometimes we were even invited to their weddings. At that time I became a big shot.

The cheapest nightgown we had was $15. We had a factory in a small town near Shanghai and we had 300 women making Chinese underwear, gowns and slips and panties. That was our main business that we imported to San Francisco, and we made a fortune at it. They were pure silk, all hand embroidered, and we sold a set, $15 a gown, $15 a slip and $7.50 a pair of panties. And people would come in and buy six sets; five sets; three sets. The Junior League, no girl at that time married without buying a set from us.

Otto didn't like me being in the store. I was very charming, they claimed, and I remembered every customer, that was the funniest thing. I remember one time a woman had come in and about two, three years later she came in again— "How do you do, Mrs. Frank" "You remember me?" I remembered them and I impressed them. That made me kind of blown up like a balloon. We're all human. Otto didn't like me in the business.

In 1929 when the big crash came you could not sell a thing. We had jade pieces for $5,000 apiece; Buddhas, the most gorgeous things. That was in 1929. We took all our merchandise into the St. Francis Hotel and that's when we went bankrupt with the merchandise that nobody bought. We had no money. All we had was a very beautiful store in the St. Francis Hotel.

The St. Francis Hotel, 1930

St. Francis Hotel Lobby, 1930

We were so dumb. When the Depression happened, a woman came into Otto's and ordered some cloth from Japan and they sold for $100-$150 apiece. She gave Otto an order for one or two of those robes; they hung them on the walls, you know. She came in and said to Otto--I'll never forget it, it was on the 29th of October--she said "I don't know if I should take them, look what's happening, people are jumping out of the windows killing themselves"—and we didn't know what she was talking about. Otto never did shares or stocks, he didn't know it was a stock crisis. At that time Otto went back to China and brought forty or fifty thousand dollars' worth of merchandise, and we paid 90% duty. And we sat with that merchandise without money.

We had sales girls in the store. Mildred was a wonderful girl. I enjoyed working in the store. I was in heaven. That's when I began to know more than Otto did. That was a terrible thing. I thought I was a better sales lady, and I thought some things that didn't sell so fast was because he bought it and I really didn't know anything. It was a very bad time.

When I look back now, I see how stupid I was. Otto was a very big businessman in China. And when I came to San Francisco, he was still the big businessman in his mind. He did not realize when he was in China, and when I was there, the Chinese were already working on communism.

The Depression and Disaster

When the Depression started in 1929, Otto went to China and he came back with about fifty thousand dollars of new merchandise and he had to pay duty on it, and we didn't know

The Temple of Heaven

The St. Francis Hotel
San Francisco, California

what the Depression meant. We were so green we didn't know what the stock market meant. We invested our last money and went bankrupt. From 1926 to 1932, we had the business in the St. Francis Hotel, and we had a very good business. Then the Hitler period started. With the Hitler period he became a Nazi, and I was a Nazi with him.

When Hitler came, we thought that he was going to make Germany a great wonderful country. We never dreamed that he would do what he did. When it became known in San Francisco among the people our business went bankrupt. Nobody wanted to buy from us. They thought that we were Nazis, and we were. And then the battle began between Otto and me because we began to see what was really going on in Germany. The propaganda in this country was against Germany, and I was in the middle.

We thought that the Treaty of Versailles was a very crooked unfair thing and that Germany had the right to become an important world power. But afterwards, from 1930 when Hitler was *Reichsfuhrer,* then he became premier and we began to be ostracized, Otto and I. Nobody came into our beautiful store. We had Chinese rugs, beautiful jade, and a gorgeous store, nobody came in; nobody bought. All at once nobody came into the store because Otto belonged to the German club, he was president of the German club, consequently we were Nazis

At that time, you did not express yourself against Hitler. And we didn't actually know what was happening except everything was going to be wonderful. And then the real truth came out, what was going on in Germany, and Otto couldn't take it. He didn't believe a word of it. And I didn't know either. I was incensed when I read it, but I didn't know

Ethel and Margot Rosaly Wiesinger
Born August, 1930

San Francisco

from the First World War. I thought, you see, the same thing has happened now.

There was no money. We sat in the St. Francis Hotel, which was the biggest hotel in California and we had two stores; we had a regular store and a basement. And the basement was filled with Chinese arts, four, five, six hundred dollars a rug. Nobody looked at them. We had to practically give them away to the May Company, selling them for half the price in order to get a little money.

Even those who still had money were afraid to spend it because we didn't know what was coming. The Depression started in October 1929 and lasted until 1933, 1934, until Roosevelt came to power. The first thing he did was close the banks. We did not know what Depression meant. We didn't even have money to pay the rent. $350 a month rent in the St. Francis Hotel and we didn't have the money.

We had to give up our shop in San Francisco, nobody bought our Chinese imports; it was terrible. We had no idea the hatred that grew up amongst friendly people. Otto was the president of the German club *(The Schlaraffia)* and half of the German club turned Nazi. The other half was anti-Nazi, and the battles were terrific.

The shop went bankrupt in 1933. We had beautiful things that cost two, three thousand dollars; nobody looked at them. All of a sudden we sat with thousands of dollars worth of merchandise but nobody came near us. They knew that we were Nazis. It was heartbreaking when we had to go into bankruptcy. We didn't have any money. All our wonderful things were auctioned off. It was a terrible disappointment.

Ethel, Margot, Otto and Edith

San Francisco, 1934
The only photo of the four of us together.

Great Advertising Sale
FOR ONE WEEK ONLY!
Large Stock of Ladies' Underwear
Imported Coolie Silk, hand embroidered
Nightgowns and Slips, $7.50   Teddies, $6
Crepe de Chine, hand embroidered
Nightgowns and Slips, $12.50 up   Teddies, $10 up
Pajamas, $19.50   Step-ins, $7.50   Bloomers, $8.50
Hand Embroidered Table Linen
Luncheon Sets—Banquet Cloths—Napkins
Guest Towels at reduced prices.

Happi Coats—$5 to $10
Haori Coats—$22.50 and up
Kimonos, Brocades, Priest Robes, Obis
A most wonderful selection at bargain prices.

Mandarin Coats $18.50 and up
Chinese Mats and Runners $1 and up
Peking Jewelry
Rings, Chains, Chokers, Armlets, Brooches.

SHOWER GIFTS, TROUSSEAUX, BRIDGE PRIZES
A rare opportunity to buy Christmas Gifts at low prices.
We keep open evenings.
OTTO WIESINGER
2918 Van Ness Ave. at Chestnut, San Francisco

ANNOUNCEMENT
Having just returned from my annual trip to China and Japan, I have for sale an unusual collection of
BROCADED PRIEST ROBES (over 100 years old), OBIS, HAORI COATS (crepe and georgette), OLD AND NEW CHINESE EMBROIDERIES, MANDARIN COATS and SKIRTS, PEKING JEWELRY, CURIOS.

Oriental Lingerie
Largest Stock in Town.
Prices very moderate. Your inspection is cordially invited.
OTTO WIESINGER
2918 Van Ness Ave.   GR aystone
(Near Chestnut Street)   0819

Advertisements Closing Out The Temple of Heaven

We didn't know what to do or where to go, and we were such strangers in this country.

There was strife between Otto and me. I was very unfair. Instead of understanding, I thought it was Otto's fault. You always blame something when you're ignorant. Then friction began. I was innocent because I was very stupid, and he was ignorant because he didn't know the American ways of Depression and all that. And I had a maid at home that I had to pay, she took care of Margot, I always had a maid. In the end she didn't get any money, but she took care of Margot. We have a German saying, "When poverty comes in through the front door love flies out through the window." The battles began softly around 1930, and then they became stronger and stronger. And they lasted about three years and I packed up my clothes and went to Los Angeles.

Otto was a very big man in Shanghai. He comes into San Francisco and he's nothing but a shopkeeper. He never dreamt that that would happen to him. It was a terrible time. *(The first time Otto played tennis in San Francisco he found that they did not have "boys" to retrieve the balls, like in China; he never played again.)*

I didn't have any money when I went to the grocer; there we sat with a store with hundreds of thousands of dollars of merchandise but no money. Then when Roosevelt came, he closed the banks. The banks were closed. You couldn't do anything, and then they were opened. There was some kind of readjustment, which I don't remember. But he was a blessing when he came. He changed everything for the better. And then I began to

Margot Rosaly Wiesinger

San Francisco, 1934

be anti-Roosevelt; he began to be so anti German. Because at that time, we were very pro-German, we thought Hitler was going to save the world. Funny isn't it.

When I think now, how little I knew. Edith was nine years old in 1926; Margot was born in 1930. Margot was an infant; I had a maid at home. We still tried to live up to the elegant status we lived in, but we had no cash.

I packed my bag and went to Los Angeles. I didn't know a soul there. Edith and Margot were alone with Otto in the big house in San Francisco and a maid to take care of them. Margot was born in 1930; this was in 1933. Margot was three years old. I left the whole thing and went to Los Angeles and didn't know why. I thought we could establish a new business in Chinese art. We were bankrupt in San Francisco. I thought with the things that we had maybe I can establish something in Los Angeles.

The Beverly Hills Hotel, 1936

In 1936, the Hotel was bankrupt and owned by the Bank of America. These wealthy widows were its only guests..

CHAPTER NINE
The Beverly Hills Hotel Gift Shop

In 1933 I passed by the Beverly Hills Hotel. I don't know what made me drive in, I never knew anything about the Beverly Hills Hotel, I'd never been in Los Angeles before but it was very pretty and I thought I would go in. I drove in with my car. I come into the lobby and the lobby was just beautiful, Persian rugs and leather furniture, just beautiful. I see a store in the lobby, an empty, long room with no doors, just gates, I think, what can that be? I go and ask and they tell me it's a store. It's vacant. And I rent that store.

I rent the store, I call up Otto and he sells the furniture in no time in San Francisco and takes the kids and joins me in Los Angeles. And that was the start in the Beverly Hills Hotel.

In the store in San Francisco, I worked with Otto in the business. That was the first time I worked in the business; and I come into the Beverly Hills Hotel. I have the picture of the guests in the Beverly Hills Hotel, nine old ladies, the only guests, and they were the only ones who came into my store. I had nothing to sell, some handkerchiefs and leftovers from the bankrupt store. They wanted to support me. They were glad there was somebody in the vacant store.

And I sold the first month in the Beverly Hills Hotel, $180. The rent for the store was 10%, so I gave the manager $18 rent. His wife said, "I told you that you could do business here." Nobody wanted the store. There were no guests there.

The Beverly Hills Hotel Gift Shop

In the meantime Otto came and we rented an apartment in Beverly Hills and I put Margot into kindergarten and Edith went to Beverly Hills High School, she was a senior.

After a while it became a little better at the store. I had to learn what to buy. Fred Astaire and his mother moved into the hotel. His mother was a Polish woman and she became very friendly with me. She began to give Margot dancing lessons because she gave them to Fred and Adele and made big dancers out of them. Little by little the manager of the hotel began to improve on it somehow. It was a very famous hotel before it went bankrupt.

What a struggle, what a struggle; my first struggle as a businesswoman. We paid $35 for an apartment, a little two-bedroom apartment in Beverly Hills, and for the first time I had no help. I always had help. All at once I had a business, I had to cook, and I had to fight with Otto. And it was a mess.

Now, sometimes when I cannot sleep thoughts come back like birds. I had to think back how stupid we both were he and I we were in a strange country and the Depression was on and he had never been in America before to do business.

It was very hard, very, very hard. And it never straightened out—doing all the work for the first time in my life. I didn't know cooking, I didn't know business, I didn't know the kind of people you have to associate with. We joined right away the German club in Los Angeles; he was right away accepted and we met a few people to associate with but it was a terrible struggle.

Edith, 1940

Photo by Stella DeMalzeville

Margot and Ethel

Otto Departs

Otto left for Germany in 1938. He picked up and went back to Germany. We stayed together in Beverly Hills until Edith graduated from high school and went to college. And that was a struggle because we didn't have the money to pay for her college. She went to UCLA in 1936.

It never happened to me to realize that there could be a division between Otto and I. We were so one that I thought I could say anything and do anything and he got disgusted and also thought he could do anything and say anything. So he got on a boat and went to Germany. I did not think Otto would come back. He was such a strong Nazi. And he never did. He died in 1956. *(Otto married twice after he left, once in New York and again in Germany. Edith and Margot visited him in 1954.)*

Otto went back to the Orient thinking he could start business again; he went to the Philippine Islands and brought Edith a graduation dress. And she still has the dress. Hand embroidered. Gorgeous. That must have been 1936. He left in 1937 for Germany and Edith went to college for one year and then married Julius. Otto was in Germany at the time. He contacted me from Germany immediately.

I don't think that I was sorry that he was gone because we were not happy together. We were not a fighting couple; we carried it inside. All of a sudden, I was free to do what I wanted. Like everybody else, we think we know it all, and I knew nothing, but I managed. I was relieved when he was gone.

Afterwards, I had many opportunities. I never dated. I never went out with another man. I never had a desire to meet somebody to marry. Never came to me, up to today.

Ethel Wiesinger

Beverly Hills, 1939

I never had a feeling that I was free, that I could go out with anybody or do anything I wanted. That thought never came to me. I was so concentrated on the business, and all at once, the people I met in my business. I stuck with Otto. He was a very lovely man. I never remarried again on account of him.

A Star Among Stars

When I was in the Beverly Hills Hotel I was a star with the movie stars. And I believed it. The Beverly Hills shop gave me glamour. When Fred Astaire came down, when Charlie Chaplin came down, Al Jolson came down, all of them and they sat down and they talked and they laughed and they smoked cigarettes and it was fun. I was so interested.

In 1938, they began to remodel the hotel and began to have more guests and I began to learn what to buy. I could have walked out of that hotel a millionaire if I had known how to handle it. Eventually, Walt Disney came in. He never went into the dining room unless he came first, into my in my shop. He'd be half an hour talking until his wife would come and say come on they're waiting for dinner. But he never bought anything. He just liked my conversation.

I did not know the things I was to keep for those people. I didn't know what to buy. And I stayed there until 1949. By that time I had learned. I had already a counter of genuine jewelry. Helen Jepson, Metropolitan opera star, saw a topaz ring. May I see that ring? And she took it out, she said how much is is? I said $400 and she said go to the desk to pay for it, and I did. I nearly died. It takes a lifetime to learn.

Edith in a Fashion Show

Beverly Hills Hotel 1938

Then I was nothing but store. I grew in it, I made money in it, and I had an awful lot of friends and I associated with them, Joan Crawford was coming all the time; Greta Garbo, Leopold Stokowski, Dorothy Lamour, Bette Davis--she was a cute girl. All of them, they all came. Jimmy McHugh, he was a great composer, he would have spent two, three hundred dollars for a little gift for somebody. So I sold him something for $25. And I thought I made a terrific deal. He bought it because I had nothing better. By that time, in my ignorance, I succeeded. But if I'd been real clever, I would have made a fortune.

Every Thursday evening Walt Disney came for dinner at the hotel because they introduced the buffet dinner. But before he went in there he would come into my shop. He was a wonderful man in my place, my place, where he could be a plain human being, not the great Walt Disney. And Leopold Stokowski. He just loved me. I don't know why. Al Jolson comes in and buys a package of cigarettes—I had divided the shop: one was the gift shop and one was the newspapers and cigarettes. Al Jolson comes in and buys a package of cigarettes. I said, won't you buy another one for the soldiers? Because I had a big glass jar, you bought one for you, he looks at me and says "Say, I just come back where I collected $150,000 for them"

Charlie Chaplin, he used to come in. He was a funny man. He never walked alone; he always had a guide. When they become famous they change. Most of the movie stars at that time came from nowhere. They came from very poor or plain backgrounds, but then they become the stars—Ingrid Bergman used to come in all the time. She was a lady to the manor born.

Ethel's Autograph Book

When I was in Beverly Hills Hotel I had all the movie stars, all of them. Joan Crawford would come in and sit for hours. What the people don't understand about the movie stars, particularly the common people, when they confront a movie star they are not the first one who does it. They don't realize they may be about the hundredth one already that confronts that movie star. All he has to do is sign his name and talk to them. He's a human being just the same as you and I. They want to be just plain people.

I have all their autographs. Dick Denning, when they were living in California, and Evelyn Ankers, I used to go for weekends and stay in their house, and then we'd go out to dinner. We always would go out for dinner. When we go to dinner he would say let's go to a corner of the restaurant where no one will see us, where we can have our dinner in peace because people would come and want an autograph always. So I had that companionship.

Fred Astaire, he was such a darling. You have no idea what a fine, simple man Fred Astaire is. He's Austrian, you know. His real name is Austerlitz. Ann Astaire, she called herself Astaire, but she came from Poland somewhere. I was a very good friend with Fred Astaire's mother, Ann Astaire. She was Viennese; her name was Austerlitz. She was a very outstanding woman, a lady to the manor born, one of the very, very few ladies. The mothers of a lot of those movie stars are very simple, plain people, very ordinary. Because most of the movie stars, some come practically from the gutter. But Fred Astaire's mother was a lady to the manor born.

There was a Mr. Hacker, but I did not associate with him. He was one of the nicest men that I could have liked.

Ethel and Margot

Beverly Hills 1938
Ethel loved to dress Margot in dirndl
dresses like a little German girl.

he used to sell jewelry and I used to buy from him. And I didn't know whether he liked me or he liked my shop. *But Er hat immer noch von sex gesprochen. (He always spoke of sex.)* He disgusted me. No, that was not the attraction. He was very good looking, highly cultured, from a very outstanding group of people in Vienna. He was a widower. I never went out to dinner with him, he asked. I did only shop business with him. He would have interested me, we were on the same level socially and educationally, in every way except that. I couldn't stand him for that. It was an insult to me, to talk to me about it. Because there were other women; there was one woman from Vienna who was an actress in Vienna and she was after him. She would have done anything, so go ahead and do it.

I was so blown up with my association with the movie world that I thought I was one of them. Al Jolson came in; I had his autograph. Those people are always under camouflage. They always have to be the great actor. Sometimes when they can take off that junky harness and be a plain person like they used to be before, they enjoy it.

Bruce Cabot was another one like that, a gorgeous, looking man. He came in one time, I used to have very expensive and very beautiful ties, men's ties. Many times when he came in he forgot his tie. So he came in and bought my ties, they were 10, 15 dollars a tie, which at that time was a lot of money. One time he comes in, he walks right over to the end and picks a tie and comes over and gives me a tie, he takes out and gives me a bill. I thought it was a $10 bill, I looked at it, it looks so funny, I looked at it again, son of a gun, he gave me a $1000 bill, to tease me. I couldn't give him change for a $1000 bill. He got such a kick out of it. He was very cute. He was so handsome.

Tante Martha, Margot and Ethel

228 Rexford Drive
Beverly Hills, California

At Home in Beverly Hills

When Otto left I got a housekeeper. Otto left in 1938. A friend of mine, her husband was a newspaper man and died; he was a big gambler and gambled all his money away and went bankrupt and she had no place to go. So I said "Martha, you come to me." So we two lived together from the time Otto left, I paid her $40 a month and she ran my house.

I worked seven days a week. It was my pleasure. It was my joy. I had a good woman at home to take care of us; if I wanted people I'd say Martha, we'll have six people for dinner today. I came home, the table was set, the dinner was cooked everything was done. I didn't even know what we were going to have.

Martha Matenaers had been the governess of the Potts family in Chicago who was in intimate association with the Rockefellers. Before Martha married she raised children who were friends of Stevenson, Adlai Stevenson. His wife and the wife of the woman that Martha worked for were intimate friends. And the McCormicks and the Rockefellers were all the group of people. She had a maid to make her bed and make the rooms in which she and the children lived. And then the children grew up. And they went to colleges.

And Mrs. Potts whom she worked for was so awful that her husband committed suicide. Martha said he was the finest man that she ever met in her life and this was the woman that she worked for. But before he did that, Mrs. Potts tried to get Martha be kind of an influence with her husband so that she would have some kind of a divorce case. And Martha knew it. Mrs. Potts came home one time with a big beaver coat for Martha, they had big afghan dogs and that she should put on that coat and go with the dogs for a walk. And people would say "This is the governess of the Potts." She said she never wore the coat. She never put it on. She was a very decent woman; a little bit dumb.

She saved some money and went to Chicago where she met a man who issued a German paper for the farmers in Chicago. He was a spendthrift, he had no money but she did not know that. So he started to flirt with her and she married and she was through with the Potts.

She married this man and she moved to Kerman, California, which is a very small village in California, and he became a *Schlaraffia,* a very exclusive German club for only prominent people. *Schlaraffia* is a land where the rivers are all made out of honey, the pigeons are flying in the air, but they are already cooked and roasted. So you open your mouth and a pigeon will come in and you eat it. There is one in Detroit. There is a beautiful *Schlaraffia* in Detroit. So Otto became the president of the *Schlaraffia* and Mr. Matenaers and Martha became members.

There was a big *Schlaraffia in* San Francisco we had a very beautiful membership. In New York, all the German opera stars belonged to the *Schlaraffia.* And when we had a meeting, they would sit and sing their heads off. And the writers: Otto could write poetry and he came from China and he was very good looking and he was a gentleman to the manor born, and he was invited to *Schlaraffia,* and that's where I met Martha. And then we became very close friends and on weekends we would drive over to Kerman and we'd stay over the weekend, and they would come to San Francisco and they would be our guests.

And then the Depression set in. We didn't know what Depression meant. 1929. Neither Otto nor I had any idea, when people talked we didn't know what they were talking about.

Mr. Matenaers started a farm of his own. And he used Martha's money to buy special cows and heifers, and have a farm of his own. He wanted to go into the breeding business but he should have known it was a depression, and the farmers who had the cows already and had the heifers went bankrupt, but he never thought about it. And he lost every cent they had. He got a stroke and died. She didn't have any money to bury him. She sold her furniture and she sold her piano and she was penniless. So she came to me. And she stayed with me for years. But she was not a servant, she was a member of the family. *(Martha said that Matenaers was sent to the San Joaquin Valley to introduce cotton as a crop, which he did.)*

My Favorites

I could not adjust to the American men. I was thoroughly German. The war was going on. There was not one man who appealed to me. But in the Second World War there was a man that appealed to me. One man. Leopold Stokowsky. Then Greta Garbo came along and took him away.

I had already my shop in the Beverly Hills Hotel and he was a guest in the Beverly Hills hotel. He was more a guest in my shop than in the hotel. I don't know what it was, there was a secret about Stokowski: he was from Polish descent and his parents were in England I don't know whether he was born in England or he was brought to England from Poland. We were in Czernowitz, in the Bukovina in the Carpathian Mountains.

Austria got a part of Poland, and they divided Poland into three parts *(1772)*. One part went to Germany, one part stayed in Russia, that's when the Jews came into Russia; there were no Jews in Russia but when Russia took over Poland they had to take over the Jews too. The reason that the Jews were in Poland was the inquisition in Spain. When the inquisition was, Poland had a very tolerant King Sobieski, Johan Sobieski *(1763)*, and he permitted the Jews when they were expelled from Spain, not all of them but whoever wanted to, to come to Poland. So when Poland was divided a part of the Jews that lived in one part went to Germany, a part went to Russia and a certain part, Galicia, was given to Austria. And they called it Galicia because there is a province in Spain by the name of Galicia, so they named that. The Emperor of Austria was very tolerant to the Poles; he permitted them to keep their Spanish language, Galician language, and Polish.

In Russia, they immediately had to turn to Russian, and in Germany they immediately had to turn to German. In Galicia they were permitted to keep their Polish language. And I think that the parents of Stokowski were in Galicia and then immigrated to England. Whether he was born in Galicia or not, I don't know. My parents had relatives in Galicia, in Krakow. So when Stokowski came in and we started to talk to get acquainted and talked of Galicia and I said my parents had relatives in Krakow he blew up. And from that time on he became very friendly. And he always wanted to know about Krakow.

So I suspect that his parents might have come from Krakow. And either he was born there and never told or was born in England but his parents remembered Krakow. He was very fond of me. And he bought a lot from me. I never went out with him. *(In Oliver Daniel's 1982 biography:* ***Stokowski--A Counterpoint of View,*** *Daniel found that Stokowski came under the influence of his first wife who for professional and career reasons "urged him to emphasize only the Polish part of his background.")*

At that time, Otto had left for Germany and I was as far removed from men as could possibly be. It never entered my mind that I could ever marry another man. It was totally out of my mind. I was happy in the shop and I met a lot of very interesting people. They all liked me and they all came in and supported me and bought and talked.

They always found I had interesting things to talk about. If they chose a topic I would always get into it and be able to talk about it with them. I never suggested anything to talk to them and they always came in with a big smile and started to talk. They got right into it. Stokowski would come over and over again. At that time it was very stylish— *Transcendentalism and the Power of the Mind*—and he went out and bought a book of the *Power of the Mind* and he came in, it was that thick, that big. And he said now I'm going to study the power of the mind. I don't know whether I instigated it or what it was. I really don't even remember what they talked to me. But they stayed for hours.

When Stokowski stayed in the Beverly Hills Hotel he lived more in my shop than in the hotel. I really don't know hotel. I really don't know why. He only bought from me. He brought in Greta Garbo who bought from me. I made her a very beautiful coat. He brought her in and then she came in alone to buy from me.

One time she talked about Stokowski. I said to her, he is so humble. Everywhere he went to and with everybody he

Edith and Julius Gilbert

Edith and Julius married in 1940. Julius was a guest in the Hotel when they met. He had come to Beverly Hills from Detroit after his divorce to undergo psychoanalysis by the famous Viennese psychiatrist, Otto Fenichel.

came in to me he talked everyday things, like we sit down and talk together here. And he relaxed from being the great Stokowski; he was just a plain ordinary man. So when I said to Greta Garbo, he is so humble, which was true, and she looks at me, she had the most beautiful eyes I have ever seen and she says "All great people are humble." And so was she, lovely. She came in never dressed up, never pretending, in a pair of shoes she had feet like that, a plain coat, looked around, we talked and then came the big affair between her and Stokowski, but it broke up. They didn't fit.

She was Swedish or Norwegian, and he was what he was, and he did not look to compete with another star. When he wanted to talk to someone he wanted to relax from stardom and that's why he came to me. I never talked about his music, I never talked about what a great man you are, we sat down and talked like we talk here, plain. It was like taking off a harness and being just a plain man. When he was with Greta, she was in a harness and he was in a harness. And they got tired of each other. He was not married. I think he was married twice, but at that time he was not married. Afterwards he was married to the Vanderbilt girl. And they couldn't stay together either. Every time he came to the Beverly Hills Hotel he came into my store. When he was there as a guest he was in my store. *(In March 1938 Stokowski vacationed with Greta Garbo on the island of Capri in Italy. This followed other reports of friendship or romance between Stokowski and Garbo. He later married Gloria Vanderbilt.)*

When Disney came in from Disneyland, he never came in without coming into my shop. We talked plain things, just likehe talked to his mother, plain things. They are tired of talking stardom. They have so much to contend with that.

I was very friendly with Dick Denning and his wife Evelyn Ankers. The mother and daughter moved into the Beverly Hills Hotel. Evelyn Ankers was a great actress in England and she was hired by Universal City to come to play the young girl in *Arsenic and Old Lace.* She came with her mother. Her mother was a very domineering woman and brought up her daughter to become a great actress and she was an actress the same as the daughter; she supported her mother of course.

After Evelyn Ankers played in *Arsenic and Old Lace,* she got a contract at Universal Studios. Universal made a contract for her to be in other plays too. And I became very friendly with the mother. The mother told me all kind of stories that I knew were a little different. She looked very common, a common English woman. And then I looked at her hands and her hands looked as if she had worked all her life very hard. They were a working woman's hands. This little girl Evelyn was very, very beautiful, and in a way very innocent. Outside of her profession as being an artist she knew very little. And she probably went through in America the same thing that I went through. Everything was so different. At that time she must have been 24, 25 years old.

There was a very famous actor, I think it was Ford, and he was with his mother, also in moving pictures. And he was about six feet tall and was the most gorgeous looking man you ever saw. And the mother was almost as big as I, I don't know if she was even as big as I, very thin and a big bitch. Terrible. She had that big great man in her hands. He had even to eat what she told him to. He was probably between 20 and 30. And he had become a big star, but scared to death of his mother. And they lived together, they lived in the Beverly Hills Hotel. She had a room, he had a room, then they bought a house and lived in a house, and that man liked Evelyn. She was very beautiful.

When I went out of the hotel they took in a real jeweler and is he cleaning up there. The jeweler is still there. Macon.

Beverly Hills Gift Shop
Ethel Wiesinger

453 NORTH BEVERLY DRIVE
BEVERLY HILLS, CALIFORNIA
PHONE • CRESTVIEW 6-5730

CHAPTER TEN

Winding Down

I supported myself since 1936 when I went to the Beverly Hills Hotel. That was the break. I became a businesswoman without knowing how to act. When I left the Beverly Hills Hotel I had two thousand dollars and I had a terrific stock but it was not the right stock for the Beverly Hills Hotel. So I opened a shop on Beverly Drive, the main street of Beverly Hills and I was glad to be out of the Hotel.

It was quite successful: the shop was beautiful and I learned. The salesmen teach you what to buy, the salesmen came in and offered merchandise. I never bought compacts, stylish compacts *(purse mirrors with powder holders)*. To buy compacts and sell them, I didn't know how and what. I think I went to school all my life, and I think I still have to go to school.

But then I got the sales girls in and I had to fight with them. I didn't fight with them but they stole me blind. I went into one sales girl's apartment with two policemen, I took out $1200 worth of merchandise. How much money she stole I'll never know. That was only one girl. I did not know what business was. Now I admit it. At the time I thought I knew it all. I was so proud to open that beautiful shop in Beverly Hills on Beverly Drive. And I knew nothing.

Lockeed Air Terminal, Burbank

A bookkeeper came to me from the Beverly Hills Hotel and told me there was an opportunity to open a shop in in the Lockheed Air Terminal in Burbank, so I opened a shop there. Two shops! I almost went bankrupt.

Ethel at Work

Lockheed Air Terminal, Burbank
1950

At the one at the airport, I took in five, six hundred dollars a day. And they stole there. One time a girl called me up and said they broke in. I had a safe; someone broke in the safe and took out $800.

I almost went bankrupt with the two shops. I had six girls, three in Beverly Hills and three in the airport. I was not capable. I was not experienced. The opportunity was there. If clever people, I mean experienced people had been there they could have made a fortune in those two shops. But I didn't know how. I wasn't trained for it. I sold the shops.

I sold them in 1954. I gave up the shop in the Lockheed Terminal and then right after that the Korean War started, and the soldiers were coming in and they spent all their salaries in the gift shop. The woman who took it over made a fortune. I had only the Beverly Hills shop and I got disgusted with that. I said I can't handle this anymore.

Real Estate

In 1954, Edith's girlfriend Jean came in to see me. Her father was in construction. They were building apartment houses; she was a very wealthy girl. She said my mother, my father and I are going to real estate school; we are taking real estate so we have the right to sell our own properties. Real estate people would come to us and say we want to sell your property. So I said, "Jean, I'll go with you." I went with them six weeks and I took the examination and I passed. I received a postal card that I passed. It came on the 24th of December. I said this is the nicest Christmas present I could have. Because everyone laughed at me, that I was taking up real estate.

The Family in Charlevoix, 1948

Edith, Ethel, Margot and Julius

I took it up because I went crazy without the business; to sit all at once at home and do nothing? So we went together and I passed the exam. I couldn't get over it. I had learned so much by being in business. I had a bookkeeper who kept my books. I learned from him from 1934 to 1943, ten years, I should have learned something.

When I lived in Beverly Hills and I had the license, I had it for six months without going into a real estate office, although I had to have a real estate office in order to pass the examination. There was a house for sale in my neighborhood and there was a sign with the real estate broker. I went to him and I asked if I could name him as my boss so I could have the real estate license. He did it, and I never sold a house in a year. I never bothered. *(Ethel had many friends who were older and when they sold their homes to down-size she would refer them to her realtor and get a finder's fee. That is how she used her license.)*

Then I went to Europe and I traveled around for three months in Europe, had the time of my life. I went every year twice to Edith, to Detroit but it was an empty life.

Charlevoix, Michigan

I had a wonderful last 40 years of my life, the last 40. The first 40 depended on my situation: my parents, Otto, my children. The last 40 everything that happened to me was my doing. Edith was gone, she is married 43 years, Margot went away to college, she married her first husband. I didn't like him. He had one job in his life, he joined the Young Men's Christian Association, he stayed there 32 years.

I've been living here in Charlevoix now for 17 years; in June will be 17 years. Here, you go to bridge parties, you don't talk about anything. They are intelligent women, they

Ethel in Venice

Ethel finally received her U.S. citizenship in 1954 after WWII. At last she could visit old friends and relatives in Europe and Israel.

are college graduates, but they don't talk about what they know. It's amazing how much one can learn from reading. You see how other people do something, either right or wrong. Either way. It's a fantastic thing. You can't live without books.

In 1975, when President Carter was meeting with Egypt President Anwar Sadat, what he and Carter accomplished in the peace treaty was the greatest thing anyone could have produced. Anwar Sadat was the greatest man of the 20th century. I started writing him and giving him advice: not to wage war against Israel. Why not? Why do people write their representatives and senators? I had nothing to lose and I think he considered my advice. I wrote "You have led your country into two losing wars. If you had used that money to build hospitals, schools, libraries, museums and orphanages, how many happier people would you have had instead of graves?" The destiny of the world was in the hands of the Middle East. It was a critical year. Sadat was the man who held the equilibrium. He never answered but sent me *Ramadan* cards. I stopped writing in 1979 with the signing of the Camp David Peace Accords. I was not surprised that Sadat was assassinated. He was living among enemies.

I was to a party here, a doctor was here, the head doctor of Charlevoix. I had a drink in my hand and he had a drink in his hand and we sat down in a corner, and the house was full of people, it was at the Rothschilds, that party, and somehow, we started to talk, and sat and talked and talked and talked. And finally he got up, his wife came and said we have to go home, and he said if nothing else, this conversation with you made it worthwhile coming to this party. That shocked me. I don't

Ethel's Charlevoix House

MRS. ETHEL WIESINGER stands near a carved Chinese chow table in her delightfully decorated Charlevoix home.

know what we talked about but a man of his stature to say to me that talking to me made it worthwhile coming to that party. It shocked me.

There is no one here to play mahjong with. And I have one woman that I play Scrabble with. They don't want to play Scrabble here. Anybody I ask to play Scrabble, they say they don't know how to spell. The woman who knitted this sweater for me is the one I play Scrabble with. She's a college graduate and a very lovely person. She works here in the hospital a lot as a volunteer, and we played three or four times Scrabble and I won every time. And she brought me this sweater and now we'll sit and play a game of Scrabble. I let her win. I didn't want to let her lose. But she really doesn't know how to play.

I think I'm blessed with a certain ability which some people are scolded for being that way. I can speak to beggars, their language. I can speak to wealthy people, their language. And I can speak to rich people their language. And to poor people their language. I don't go into the hospital and say "Hello, how are you, I'm feeling so good today." Would you say that?

You have to know to whom you speak. You don't have to agree with them and say you are very right and not wrong. You don't have to do what they do or believe what they do. But you can have a conversation with them. There's a Chinese saying: the Chinese don't like to go to court because the judge is often the relative of one of the parties, the defendant or the accuser. And he is not going to accuse his relative. So they don't like to go to court; they have arbitration. They will take five people or seven people or nine people or three people and they will settle with them, whatever they have to do. Because a judge will say you are absolutely wrong what you say to the accuser but he is not wrong either.

The kids today will live in a different world. Someday I'll sit in a cloud and flap my wings and say "I told you so."

You look backwards and don't remember a lot of things. I was always a pet, but didn't know it. My mother was 86 when she passed away in 1933, My father was 76 when he passed away in 1920. I was in Europe when my father passed away. I was already married in 1920 and Otto and I went to visit his father after the war.

I enjoy every day of my life now because I have no responsibilities. I can live from day to day and enjoy the sunshine and the moving of the trees. You sit here and it's like paradise. And the leaves are beginning to come in on the branches, and once in a while there is a little bird that comes. I'm very lucky.

I have a good day today. I enjoy every day if I stay the way I am. I can hear and I can see and I can talk and I can walk. I cannot walk long distances now but I can walk and take care of my house, and enjoy parties, I had a bridge game last night and we had so much fun. I enjoy my life today more than when I was very young because when I was very young I had all kinds of responsibilities. Now I don't have any. I just live on and am very happy and very grateful.

Family Stories

Ethel Wiesinger

Beverly Hills, 1959

An Atypical Thanksgiving

As told to Walter Smith

(Freely transcribed and updated from a letter I read when I was 11 from Ethel Wiesinger. I was also there at age four. This happened around 1957. Ethel was my grandmother.)

Hello Darling,

I know I haven't written as often as I should, so I hope all is well with you and your family. I just wanted to let you know the Kate is out of the emergency room and the grandkids are not harmed at all, with little effects from the Thanksgiving day adventures.

Darling, let me tell you about our Thanksgiving. It was to be a small affair, with myself, Margot, Jerry and the two grandkids, Walter, age four and Janet, age two, and Jerry's mother and Grandmother.

I ordered a small Turkey from the butcher. We began making the apple strudel and stuffing early. Margot and the kids showed up with the fruit wine jello and the marshmallow candied yams. Margot picked up Ola and Sally, Jerry's mother and grandmother, in Ethel's car, which had real estate signs stored in the back seat. When she turned a corner, the signs fell over and hit Grandma Sally on the nose, giving her a cut. This caused quite a stir when they arrived.

Margot tried to help with the food, but she is just terrible in the kitchen and soon they were all relaxing in the living room. Soon there was a knock on the door and who do you think it was but my nephew Jules Gilbert and his family, wife Ruth and daughter Caroline. They came through the door and said they could not stand for me to spend

All Together at Thanksgiving, 1958

Janet and Walter

Grandma Ethel and Turkey

Aunt Jeanette

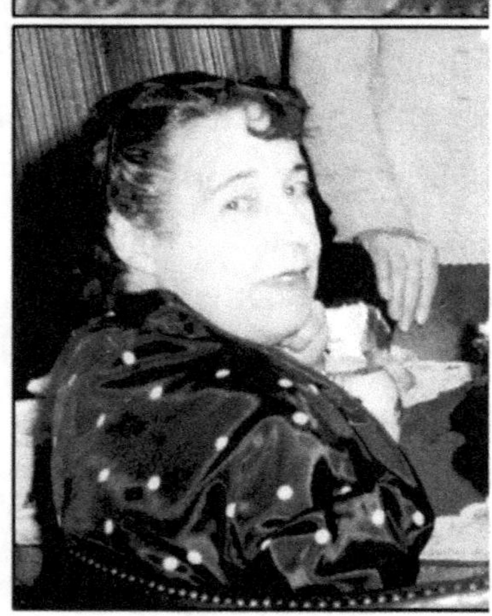

Grandma Ola

Great Grandma Sally

Thanksgiving alone. As usual, they brought nothing, and I started to add some more flour to the strudel and bread to the stuffing.

I was cooking in the kitchen and everybody was getting loud in the living room. I noticed the kids racing around like a flock of wild geese but thought nothing of it. They were running from one end of the house to the other, out through the kitchen door, to the yard and back into the house in the front door. We could bring no order. When the turkey was ready I called the families to set the table and wash for dinner.

Margot went to the restroom to wash up and found the door locked. She waited and waited and finally knocked. No answer. She knocked some more. No answer. Then we noticed Walter and Janet were missing. She pounded on the bathroom door and heard a low moan inside. As we walked to the living room to discuss the situation we noticed the wine Jello. The kids had opened it and picked out all the cherries and grapes. They had all gotten drunk and ran around like a herd of elephants before falling asleep.

Walter and Janet had locked themselves in the bathroom, thinking they were in trouble for ruining the Jello. They had fallen asleep on the bathroom floor. Margot continued to pound on the door. Finally the kids woke up and told us they had thrown the key to the locked door out the bathroom window, so no one could get in to punish them. Each of us in turn, tried to pick the lock to no avail. One tried a knife, one tried a bobby pin, safety pin and so on, but the lock was too stiff. By then it was dark, so we all took candles and went out onto the lawn to look for the key.

While we were looking, a limousine pulled up and who got out, but my sister-in-law Jeanette and her sister Kate!!! They were back from their cruise through the Panama Canal, dressed in their finest clothes and furs. While on board ship, Kate had fallen and broken her arm, and needed to go to the doctor. I did not know what to do, and in the end an ambulance came and took her to the emergency room.

When Kate and Jeanette arrived, what a sight it was. Five grown people, dressed for Thanksgiving Dinner, on their hands and knees with candles looking for the key in the grass. The driver put their trunks and bags from the cruise in the living room. Jeannette and the driver proceeded to help look for the key. Finally we gave up. Jules tried to open the bathroom window and climb through to unlock the door from the inside. The window was too small. Jules could not climb through, nor could the ladies. Aunt Jeanette had the idea to call cousin Caroline. She was 14 and petite. We kept talking to the kids in the bathroom but they did not make any sense, and were barely awake. They could not unlock the door and thought they were in terrible trouble no matter how we reassured them.

Caroline, age 14 was happy to climb through the window and open the door. Jerry and Jules lifted her to the window and put her through. As she braced her arm against the sink the pedestal gave way and down she went. She hit the floor and the bath tub and then crawled over to the door, across the wet floor from the damaged sink and unlocked the latch handle. We pulled the kids out. Jerry and Jules worked on abating the water gushing from the broken pipe on the sink. Meanwhile, we thought the best thing to do would be to get something in the kid's stomach while we were waiting for the ambulance to pick up Kate. Dinner was ready and we gave them a couple of rolls.

The children were fine, after all. We all were in the living room, everyone hungrily looking at the turkey. I looked at the ambulance driver and the assistant and asked "Have you had any Thanksgiving turkey?" They shook their heads "No." So I looked at my small turkey, and all the people, and again at my small turkey, and said "Lets all have a wonderful Thanksgiving dinner." We all sat wherever we could find a space, and somehow everyone got something to eat. The turkey dinner for seven ended up feeding 15 People. Everything was superb.

Kate went to the hospital emergency room to get her wrist set and is now back home. Jules left with his family in that huge car he is so proud of, but when they got home to their estate in San Fernando Valley, though, someone had driven through the front electric gate--what a shock! Ola and Sally were given a ride home. Margot, Jerry and the kids spent the night on the couch. I gave some strudel for the ambulance drivers to take with them. Jeannette is in the guest bedroom. It is now three in the morning, and I thought I would drop you a line before I retired.

Love,
Ethel

Ethel, Otto, and Edith

Hankow, China, 1925

My Shanghai – At Age Seven

Edith Gilbert

A fancy poster in the lobby of a swank New York hotel hawked the display of world famous Hong Kong tailors; it brought to mind a hand-printed sign I saw in a little Shanghai tailor shop *"Ladies may have fits upstairs."*

Long forgotten memories of that far away tailor shop sparked a series of vignettes. That China was no ordinary country first impressed me, oddly enough, on the opposite side of the world, in Hamburg, Germany. It was 1923; I was six years old and Mother and I were visiting grandfather in Deutschland. Inflation raged and the value of money had lost all its meaning. People were trading silverware for groceries, antique bric-a-brac for a pail of milk.

Walking to the dairy store with our empty pails, mother chatted about the letter she'd received that day from Daddy in Shanghai. He enclosed boat passage and urged us to join him at once. In contrast to Germany, business conditions in China were good.

"When we arrive in Shanghai, Ditchen, you will start school" mother said cheerfully as we stepped into the cool, clean milk depot. We'd made the crossing from New York to Hamburg three times before I was six years old, and the thought of another boat trip delighted me, but the prospect of school was definitely unsettling. In my temporary quandary, I was shaken by loud shrieks of dismay that burst forth from Hilda, the German dairymaid, when she heard mother was taking me to Keena, as she pronounced China "How can you take this sweet, blue-eyed child to live among those heathens?" Hilda wailed, flinging and rocking me in her ample breasts until another customer arrived and I was mercifully released.

This was my first recollection that China was a special kind of place and from that day on, I precociously announced to everyone we met that I was going to China, but by then our friends and neighbors must have already heard the news because never again was I met with such an emotional outburst.

A great deal of discussion followed as to which direction we should take to Shanghai: east, via the Suez Canal, or west, via America, and I remember going to sleep listening to the adults arguing pro and con. If anyone had asked me, I'm sure I would have voted for the Suez Canal, Even at that tender age it sounded more romantic and after all, I'd already been in America. But America won.

We sailed from Hamburg on a beautiful summer day, waving frantically from the ship's rail to friends, whom we'd never see again. The lively, sentimental tunes of a swinging German band played *Liebe Heimatland, Adieu a*nd we headed out to sea.

Somehow the trip to New York across the United States to San Francisco made no impression on me, for I cannot recall anything until we boarded the Japanese liner, the Korea Maru, for Shanghai and sailed west through the Golden Gate. I remember mother packing summer dresses for me and saying that the weather was going to get warmer and warmer as we approached Honolulu. I was intrigued by the Japanese sailors quiet efficiency, by the sukiyaki dinners served on deck to passengers squatting on straw mats over small hibachi stoves long after I was supposed to be asleep. I had the run of the ship and spent long hours in the pilot house listening to the tapping communiqués going over the old wireless and at times, when the sea was calm, stood quietly beside the captain as he steered the huge ship into the tropical setting sun.

But most of all I remember watching the wake of the ship for hours as the sun played on the ever changing forms. As the days grew warmer, there was more and more talk of Diamond Head. It was disappointing to a girl my age when we pulled along the huge, plain gray rock called Diamond Head in the harbor of Honolulu. I'd expected to see a flashing, fiery brilliant diamond beacon set against a blue sky and blue water.

Once ashore, disappointment fled. The exotic flowers, the bright mumus, the cheerful plucking of ukuleles, the fresh green grass skirts keeping rhythm with the waving palms, the wonderful white beach, the juicy sun-ripened pineapples were overshadowed only by the thrill of ascending the falls where King Kamehameha chased his opposing army to their destruction over that sheer high cliff.

On this cliff, for the first time in my life, I stood above thick, billowing cotton candy clouds. Clouds I wanted to walk on, to roll through, to play hide and seek in, but Mama said "No." So down the mountain we drove in a black Ford touring convertible, lost in reverie at what might have been. Until we arrived at the Honolulu Museum where we saw the royal cape made of thousands of tiny yellow feathers which once belonged to great King Kamehameha and I wondered if his mother would let him walk on clouds.

As we approached the International Date Line the ship's talk centered around the lost day. We were going to have Tuesday then Thursday and old timers were initiating

Edith on Board the Korea Maru, 1924

new passengers with timeless pranks and stunts that have always been associated with this odd event.

Occasionally we would see another boat sailing slowly by on the horizon but usually there were long quiet days, uninterrupted by the clubhouse atmosphere of today's luxury cruises. Taking a turn around the deck, long conversations at the rail, reading in deck chairs were the general pastimes between meals.

Finally we reached Japan. We went ashore for a day in Kobe, in Yokohama, in Kyoto. The presence of crowds of people, the narrow cobblestoned streets, the bright temples and strange smells must have exhausted me as I remember dozing off and being gently carried up the gangplank home. The Korea Maru was home to us for twenty-eight days. Twenty-eight days from San Francisco to Shanghai.

I'll always remember Papa waiting for us on the pier when we arrived. I had never seen him in British walking shorts before. He looked very elegant in his sport jacket, carrying a cane, but those shorts on my Papa! He stood smiling and waving at us among the tremendous bustle of customs officials, sailors, vendors, stevedores and visitors, for in those days half the foreign colony came to meet the boat.

We picked our way through the bales and lines and crates; with a great deal of shouting in Chinese we found a rickshaw that took us to Papa's bachelor apartment. Mama took one look at the apartment and I knew we weren't going to stay there long. It was so dark.

I have no recollections of the surroundings at all. When mother suggested I needed a bath, the "boy" placed a brown wooden tub in the middle of the room. A coolie was

Our Third Floor Apartment

hailed from the street below and for a few coppers he carried the pails of hot water upstairs for my bath.

The next few days were spent house hunting. The first time I saw our new home I fell in love with it. It was in the French section on Avenue Joffre, a huge mansion with beautiful grounds and a tennis court. The house had been divided into three large apartments: the first floor was occupied by an English couple; the second floor by a French couple; the third floor apartment was to be ours. Mother was busy with painters, carpenters and plumbers, rearranging the kitchen, enlarging a room here and dividing a room there. We finally moved into our spacious, cheerful new home the same day I was enrolled in school.

There was no question as to which school I was going to attend. Since my parents were German I was enrolled in the

Kaiser Wilhelm Schule. If my parents had been American, I would have been enrolled in the American school; or if they'd been English in the British school, or if they'd been French in the French School.

It wasn't long before I could tell by the uniforms the boys and girls wore what their nationality was, which church they attended and at which club their parents played tennis or bridge.

Before starting school, mother took me to a shoemaker where my shoes were made to order. The whole time we lived in Shanghai I never had a pair of store-bought shoes, much to my regret. I also needed a special cap; each child in Kaiser Wilhelm wore one. Each grade had a distinguishing color around the edge of the cap; the boys had visors, girls none.

I don't remember if I began school on opening day or not. My parents never put much store in getting me to school on time as most of my American friends now do. I remember the bright, cheerful classrooms with perhaps a dozen pupils, the handsome young teacher Herr Ritterbusch, the strict discipline he invoked. We sat with feet together and hands folded and we learned. Our hot sweaty little hands clutched enormous pencils as we bent over lined paper while Herr Ritterbusch paraded up and down the aisles watching every "i" dotted and 't' crossed. He had a ruler and he used it. In spite of his discipline, I liked everything about the school until we started arithmetic, but I doubt if that had anything to do with Herr Ritterbusch, his ruler or the school. It had everything to do with me. Arithmetic and I are like fire and water. We just don't mix.

Edith at Kaiser Wilhelm Schule, 1925.

I never would have learned multiplication tables if I hadn't been visiting overnight with my best friend and we both came down with whooping cough. The mothers decided we might as well keep each other company while we convalesced. Inge and I were drilled daily by her conscientious mother to learn the German multiplication table but since my German has become rusty, so has my multiplication.

I went to school in a rickshaw. Coolies used to fight for my patronage because I was little and easy to pull. They trotted light-footedly, keeping rhythm with their sing-song, passing other rickshaws weighted down with stout women or hefty men. A lot of shouting went on between the coolies, sometimes they joked and sometimes they cursed each other or the white devil in Chinese. Fist shaking was common, but when a man was spit upon, watch out! This was a serious insult and usually led to a fight.

Sometimes Papa used to pick me up at school in his Chandler, an ancient bewitched car. We never knew when it would go and if it did, why. Papa bought it because it was large and had a beautiful interior of highly polished wood and genuine leather upholstery. The exterior was a magnificent maroon with great black fenders standing guard over four huge wire wheels. Mother said that father never looked under the hood when he bought the beautiful, temperamental Chandler.

Finally Papa gave up the battle and arrived at school one day driving an Overland. I was a small compact new smelling American car with scratchy upholstery, but even though the Overland was reliable and seldom let us down we never felt an attachment to it the way we did toward the tempestuous Chandler.

Even then, young as I was, I developed what I called my "lucky" or "unlucky" days. My "unlucky" days were when I encountered a certain beggar who lived in our neighborhood. Oh, everyone was used to packs of beggars following us about pleading with outstretched hands for coppers but this was a very special beggar. I remember the sense of deep shock I felt the first time I saw a human being so handicapped. He had no legs, no legs at all. He slid along the ground by pushing himself with powerful arms on a small platform that was mounted on roller skate wheels. Besides having no legs he had no ears. Instead, where his ears should have been there was pink, shiny flesh reaching from the end of his eyebrows almost halfway around the back of his head. Nor did he have any hair. I felt tremendous compassion for this poor soul and often speculated on how this condition came about. Was it by birth or by accident? Yes, those "unlucky" days when I encountered this unfortunate beggar cast a gloom over the entire day.

Edith, Otto and Ethel

Shanghai, 1925

Weekends were very special in Shanghai. The social life was gay and carefree. Many Sundays were spent at the German club where we lunched on the veranda overlooking the tennis courts. Sometimes for a change we would watch a polo game or a paper hunt as guests of our English friends.

Best of all was when papa invited mother and me to lunch at the Majestic Hotel. We always had a table by the window where we could see the colorful crowds rushing by, men and women of all nations, sailors from every port, costumes ranging from the finest brocades to the roughest homespun. Pigtails swinging gaily as old mandarins shuffled by in their black pumps, their hands folded in wide sleeves.

The contrast inside the ballroom where we were seated was great. Here all was serene, hushed. Thick carpets muffled the sound as educated voices spoke a dozen tongues, all discussing the day's affairs of business, politics and international news events. Soft music beckoned couples who gracefully waltzed on the parquet floor around a splashing fountain. I adored watching some of the elegantly groomed, fragrant Chinese women in their bright Hong Kong dresses. They were so slim, so serene, so fragile.

But best of all I loved the pastry cart! At the end of the meal the head waiter would wheel the cart heaped with exquisite French pastry by our table. There was the moment of great decision! Should I try the éclair, which I admired or one of those little fruit tarts which I'd never tasted before? Perhaps a napoleon? Or baba au rhum? "Come now, you can't take all day!" Somehow a decision was made, Papa paid the check and I floated into the lobby of the Majestic Hotel out into the bustling, noisy, crowded street filled with humanity, bicycles, wheelbarrows, chickens and automobiles.

As everyone knows, good help in the Orient was available and cheap. We always had German-speaking help, whereas our neighbors downstairs had French and English-speaking help. I use the terms loosely because the common language always was pidgin English, a mixture of Chinese, English, French, Portuguese and German, Italian, Japanese etc. I never needed to learn Chinese. Pidgin English sufficed.

Not only did our help speak German but the cook also had been trained to prepare typical German dishes such as *sauerbraten, wiener schnitzel* and Berliner *pfannkuchen.*

Our Number One boy always kept plenty of cold beer on hand for Papa's friends, while on the second floor the Number One Boy uncorked French wines for the guests and on the first floor the Number One Boy knew how to mix a mean scotch and soda.

Mother, God bless her, was not meant to rule over a Shanghai household. Even though Papa explained and explained the rigid formalities in dealing with our Chinese help, mother never quite seemed to get it. For example, even I knew that when I wanted something I asked the Number One Boy (if my amah wasn't around) and he would relay the message to the Number Two Boy or to the cook or gardener or chauffeur, as the case may be. Mother consistently was in hot water with our Number One Boy because she would bypass him and speak directly to the Number Two Boy. This would cause the Number One Boy to lose face and he would be forced to quit.

We were never without an amah to look after me. The first amah had bound feet. The poor thing couldn't get around very well and I was delighted when mother interviewed a broad-faced, smiling Chinese woman with big feet to replace her. Now I had someone to run and play with in the park. We children spent a lot of time in the park rolling hoops and riding bicycles while our amahs would sit on the benches exchanging bits of gossip and plucking hair off each other's forehead with a piece of string. It was intriguing to watch how deftly they handled the taut piece of string and with a twist of the wrist, a quick pull, left the forehead smooth and hairless.

Occasionally on a rainy, dull afternoon I would sneak down the back stairs where a lively mahjong game was in full swing. A week's wages were easily won or lost in an afternoon, for the Chinese delight in gambling. Sometimes I wandered into the kitchen and visited the cook who taught me a few choice Chinese phrases. Whenever the cook had visitors, he would ask me to repeat those phrases whose meaning I never understood and his friends would be thrown into gales of laughter. Fortunately, he warned me never to use my knowledge on the street and I was smart enough to follow his advice or goodness knows what may have happened.

We once had a cook who used to make the most marvelous light dumplings which were Papa's greatest joy. He bragged all over Shanghai about our cook's dumplings and one day he said to mother, "Why don't you find out how Hans (They even affected German names) makes those delicious dumplings.?" I had watched Hans for many hours with wide eyed fascination while he mixed and rolled the dough then plopped the fluffy white balls into boiling water producing his magnificent dumplings but never realized the commotion it would cause when mother discovered Hans dipped dough in flour and shaped the dumplings by rolling them under his freshly washed armpits.

Another source of never-ending friction between mother and the cook centered over the business of "cumshaw" or kickback. Everyone who has ever lived in the Orient knows that cumshaw is an established way of life; everyone, that is, except my mother. Again and again she would become incensed when she discovered evidence that the green grocer or the egg man or the fruit peddler was working in collaboration with the cook and the Number One Boy in what she considered was against her best interests.

Then she would vow to do the marketing herself. We'd march forth with a shopping list and select a dozen bananas. Mother would count each one, watch carefully while they were weighed, observe the clerk as he placed them in her basket and when she returned home she would be crestfallen as she counted eleven bananas. She'd swear never to return to that vendor but the same thing would be repeated the next day at another stand, until she threw up her hands in despair and again turned the marketing over to the smiling cook.

Occasionally the routine of our lives was broken by short vacations to the seashore resort of Tsingtau during Easter week, or Hankow, a beautiful mountain resort. Papa enjoyed showing me the fortifications of Tsingtau where he fought for the Germans in World War I, and where he was captured by the Japanese. He took me down into musty wet walled dugouts and showed me the abandoned rusty camouflaged cannons still standing.

He was very proud of the fact that he had volunteered his services to his fatherland in that far removed corner of the world, although there are few aware today that there was even a skirmish going on over there in the Far East.

The reason I remember Hankow is because we traveled to this picturesque village by sedan chair. It was fun bouncing along the narrow mountain trail, up, up, up, swinging along between two husky coolies. I never realized until years later the implications of harnessing human labor as transportation, although mother tells me now that when my Grandfather arrived in China he refused to ride in a rickshaw. He felt it was an indignity to be pulled by another human being.

I spent time in Hankow wandering through bamboo forests, picking flowers or strolling beside a clean mountain stream looking for four leaf clover or skipping across half-moon bridges and back again over flagstones placed neatly in the water.

Looking back, I seem to have had a tremendous amount of freedom to roam and explore whatever caught my fancy. There were no camps, no playgroups, no scouts, no organization except school.

There was a certain amount of regimentation of our daily lives for survival. One HAD to sleep under mosquito nets during the summer months; one could NOT drink water or milk that hadn't been boiled. One could NOT eat raw, uncooked fruits of vegetables. One was in constant fear of blood poisoning, a disease that regularly depleted the ranks of the foreign colony.

In spite of these drawbacks, it was with profound regret that I finally said goodbye to Shanghai. Many social, economic and political changes have taken place since 1925, sweeping away the lively foreign colony right along with the English sign on the tailor shop, *"Ladies may have fits upstairs."*

Our Beverly Hills Hotel
Edith Wiesinger *(1939)*

No matter where you live or what your walk in life, there is no doubt that you have heard of the Beverly Hills Hotel. President Coolidge stayed here when he toured the West Coast as have the Roosevelt's in more recent years.

There are pictures in every movie magazine of the latest starlet photographed in a latex bathing suit sitting on the diving board at the pool. Tennis enthusiasts watch Vines and Perry play exhibition matches on one of the Championship courts. And in the Sunday Society column there is apt to be an announcement that Mrs. Dillingsworth receiving after the ceremony at the Beverly Hills Hotel. Southern California dog lovers wander about the well-kept lawns at the semi-annual Dog Show, and in the sports sections twice a year a series of basketball and football teams are mentioned as resting up in this secluded out-of-town hotel before the game.

Authors from all over the world stop here while entangled in negotiating contracts with one of the movie studios. More than one has described in an article the quiet peace, the tall palms along the drives and their fictitious characters who stop at the Polo Bar just off the lobby for the required farewell cocktail. Guests are always told that Romberg composed the beautiful *"Desert Song"* in one of the private bungalows on the grounds.

I landed in this mecca of loveliness exactly five years ago when my mother opened her gift shop off the lobby. The rent then was on a percentage basis. The whole idea was an experiment which it still is, except that now the rent is no longer on a percentage based on sales. We now have a lease and pay a good rent. Nobody thinks the lease is worth very much since the hotel is so old that it is referred to as a "firetrap" and all the new guests say, "One of these days," and the old guests shake their heads in accord. But I guess when you get to be 70 or 80 years of age, "One of those days "does not sound so threatening.

Visitors who are shown around the grounds often say "Why not tear this old building down and build a beautiful modern hotel?" And then we reply, "Well, you see there is a franchise in existence that states if this hotel is torn down, it cannot be rebuilt because it is located in what is now a strictly residential district. The present solution is to modernize a little bit at a time. Look here, that was just completed."

At the Beverly Hills Hotel, as in Gaul, everything is divided into three parts. There are the guests, the staff and the shopkeepers. This distinction is as clear as the caste system in India. There is, in addition, one more "untouchable " class and that is the people who wander in for one reason or another and who are not guests at the hotel. They find themselves asked more than once, "Are you staying at OUR hotel?" When these unfortunates admit that are not, there is an immediate feeling of restraint--an awareness followed by complete disregard. It's the British attitude, "They don't belong" more than anything else I can think of. The unfortunates sense this feeling for they immediately apologize and go on to explain just what it is they are doing waiting in the lobby at three o'clock on a sunny afternoon.

The guests at the Beverly Hills Hotel are a very small group closely related to God. To displease one of them is sinful and the punishment severe. The "did you hear" episodes usually run like this: A guest complains to the manager. The complaint is immaterial and the gravity with which it is treated depends on two things. First, how much the guest is paying for the room, and second, is the complainant a permanent guest or only here for a brief stay.

In extreme cases, the offender is called into the manager's office during the daily conference and is dressed down in front of his fellow workers. Naturally this is most embarrassing especially since the particular story has already travelled the length and breadth of the corridors, and everyone has taken one side or the other. Of course, the story has lost nothing in the telling and these little episodes keep everyone, guest and staff and shopkeepers on one side of the fence or the other until the next episode when new sides are chosen.

"I can't imagine what is keeping Mr. Harris, he said to meet him here in the lobby at three," wails a plump little lady. And then she goes on, "Tell me, my dear, is the hotel full? I don't see anybody around." To which I reply for the one-thousandth time, "Yes, they are turning guests away. But of course, no matter how full the hotel is, you never see anyone around. It's especially quiet now but it will liven up around teatime." "Ooh," says the little lady, "Do they serve TEA in the afternoon?" The inflection on the work TEA is same as if I had said crocodile broth. Thank heaven, here comes Mr. Harris and the little lady waddles over to him and he quickly escorts her outside to his car. Hm. The next time he stops by the shop I must ask him who that was.

Edith and Julius Gilbert

Edith and Julius married in 1940. Julius was a guest in the Beverly Hills Hotel where they met.

Name Dropping
Edith Gilbert

When I arrived in provincial Detroit as a bride in 1940 from Beverly Hills, California, and the subject turned to music, I might mention in passing that I had worked for Leopold Stokowski, while he was making the movie *"100 Men and a Girl"* starring Deanna Durbin, and while also courting Greta Garbo.

Or, if the subject turned to literature, I might fondly remember the time that I spoke with Nobel prize winning author Thomas Mann in the lobby of the Beverly Hills Hotel, and he kindly autographed his book for me. Or if the subject under discussion was the motion picture industry, I recalled with pleasure speaking at length with the charming and renowned director, D. W. Griffith. If Walt Disney's name came up, I might enjoy telling the story of how on Thursday nights, which was cook's night out, Walt Disney used to duck out of the hotel dining room, to avoid the Congo dancing lessons given by Arthur Murray, and come instead into my mother's Gift Shop, off the lobby of the Beverly Hills Hotel. My mother was a great conversationalist and charmer, and here we would visit at length, until he was regularly paged by one of the bellboys at the request of Mrs. Disney. Then he would laugh and say with a wave of his hand, "Got to go now!"

It wasn't long before I was accused of name-dropping, which I found terribly embarrassing. This curious attitude was just the opposite of the guests staying at the Hotel. They were keenly interested in who had just checked in or out, and we were supposed to share this information.

The Maharajah of Kapurthala

The guest book in my mother's Gift Shop records many names of men and women, who have reached international fame from many walks of life. I didn't meet all of them while I attended UCLA, but I did enjoy meeting many prominent guests, and that included the Maharajah of Kapurthala It was fun asking him questions about India, which prompted him to invite me to visit him and he even promised me my own elephant! Of course, I thought this was just too funny.

The life style then, you must realize, was far more relaxed than it is today. Tea was served every afternoon in the spacious lobby and it was the hostess's duty to introduce people to each other. There were no paparazzi around to bother Spencer Tracy, while he was living with Katherine Hepburn, or to stalk Paulette Goddard, even during the scandalous lawsuit with Charlie Chaplin.

It was in the late thirties that Basil Rathbone at the height of his popularity decided there should be a charity fundraiser at the Beverly Hills Hotel. He envisioned transforming the sunny swimming pool and adjoining tennis court, both of which are surrounded by Royal Palm Trees, into an authentic Bavarian Village, of all things—a village covered with deep powdered snow! I don't remember which studio provided the snow making machine, but darned if they didn't pull it off! I'll never forget bumping into Rathbone as he ran up and down the stairs, two steps at a time, checking on every last detail. The charity affair was both a huge financial and social success and marked the beginning of a trend in fundraisers that has lasted until today.

It wasn't just at the Beverly Hills Hotel that one would run into movie stars. I was fortunate to be invited to the opening of the Racquet Club in Palm Springs one weekend during spring break. It was a warm and starry night by the pool. A small group, including Jack Powell and Bette Grable, sang familiar songs around the upright piano, just like one might do at any family cookout.

Mike Romanoff, Hedda Hopper in her hats, Clark Gable, Groucho Marx, all were walking down the street or shopping at the drug store. In looking back, I'm afraid I took this all for granted. But I hope that others will enjoy my reminiscences.

Edith Gilbert

My Book:
All About Parties, 1968

My Life Story

Edith Gilbert *(2005)*

I happened to be born in Manhattan, in the good old USA, but I could have been born in Shanghai or Hamburg just as easily!

My parents met in Shanghai before World War I. My father Otto Wiesinger had been sent to China to represent the German Dye Trust, I. G. Farben and Co. and to introduce indigo dye to China. My mother Ethel had traveled to Shanghai with her parents to visit a sister and my parents met through the German *Verein* (Association). Subsequently my mother and her parents left the Orient and settled in New York where another sister lived.

When World War I broke out, my father, still in Shanghai, volunteered to serve in the German Army to fight against the Japanese in Tsingtau.

After the war, my father looked up my mother in New York and they were married in 1916. I was born on their first anniversary in 1917. Times were difficult for Germans in the United States during these post war years, jobs were scarce and there were restrictions--for example, Germans were not allowed to go out after 6 o'clock in the evening. When I was 2½, my mother and I went to Hamburg, Germany to visit my grandfather, Karl Wiesinger, who insisted that I be baptized Lutheran. We returned again when I was a little older, booking passage on the Majestic, which was a beautiful boat. In those days, there was a great deal of fanfare before departing port; bands played and people threw colorful streamers from the deck to those on the docks.

By this time I was speaking both English and German. In 1924 my mother and I traveled from Hamburg across the United States by train to San Francisco and on to Shanghai to be reunited with my father who had started his own very successful import export business. Finally at age seven, I started school! My mother's excuse for this late start was that she felt travel was broadening!

For the next four years, I attended the *Kaiser Wilhelm Schule* in Shanghai. We wore uniforms and caps with shiny visors. At home our life style was very up scale with lots of help. I had my own amah with bound feet, who waited on me hand and foot. I wasn't even allowed to pour myself a glass of water!

In 1926 civil war broke out in China and my father's business went downhill. My mother and I left for San Francisco arriving on Dec. 24 to visit my mother relatives.

For the next four years I attended *Notre Dames des Victoires* run by the Sisters of St. Joseph. I was very happy there and got pretty good grades, but when it came time to go to high school, I decided to attend a large public school, Galileo High School in San Francisco.

My parents had started a business out of their home selling fine embroidered linens and oriental art to San Francisco's socialites. They did so well, that they decided to open a store in the beautiful St. Francis Hotel. Then came the terrible stock market crash of 1929! In retrospect it seems my parents were always in the wrong place at the wrong time!

No one had money to buy jade or hand embroidered banquet cloths and they had to give up the store down town. It was during the heart of the depression in 1930 when my little sister Margot was born.

I had just completed my junior year at Galileo High School when my parents decided to move to Beverly Hills, which was very hard on me. I had made a lot for friends at Galileo and was used to go dancing almost every weekend at one of the top hotels listening to the big bands–Glen Miller, Eddie Duchin, and Benny Goodman. Nobody, (certainly not the children of movie stars), paid much attention to this new student at Beverly Hills High School, but I did get invited to the senior prom!

By this time my parents opened a gift shop off the lobby in the Beverly Hills Hotel, which was then still in receivership. The rent was only 10% commission! The first month my mother sold $180 and the manager of the hotel said, "I told you, Mrs. Wiesinger, you would do well!"

I used to help my mother in the store while attending UCLA, and then Sawyer's School of Business where I learned to type. It was fun hanging around the Hotel because there were always interesting celebrities to talk to, including people like Walt Disney and the Maharajah of Karpurtala, who invited me to visit him in India, promising me my own elephant! Of course, I thought this was just too funny!

One day in 1938, I spotted a youngish man at the front desk. When I asked the hostess, "Who is that?" she replied, "Oh, he is an industrialist from Detroit." The "industrialist" turned out to be Julius Gilbert. We met over tea in the lobby and subsequently played tennis and swam in the new pool at the hotel. We were at the opening of the famous Polo Lounge just off the lobby. I enjoyed his company and re-assured my mother that "We are just friends!"

Fashionable Edith Gilbert, 1940

John Fredericks Hat, Suit by Adrian
Beverly Hills Couture

When Julius returned to the hotel in the fall of 1939, he was newly divorced and we started to date. He took me to the Trocadero, Ciro's, and the finest restaurants on Sunset strip. Julius proposed to me over lunch in the Brown Derby!

We were married in the spring of 1940 in Santa Monica, California. We left on the Super Chief for Detroit and moved in with his parents who lived in a three-story mansion on Arden Park, with lots of live-in help. We spent four summer months every year in our own home on Park Avenue in Charlevoix. Julius' children, Jay and Patsy, and my sister Margot, lived with us as children during much of the summer. Here we enjoyed tennis, golf, boating, swimming and far too many cocktail parties. It was a good life!

In Detroit, during World War II, I volunteered for the American Red Cross, and later attended The Society of Arts and Crafts, where I studied sculpture for four years under Walter Midener. After the war, we traveled to Florida and California and I also visited my sister and her children in Honolulu.

In 1961 Julius decided to build the Lodge Motel and we moved permanently to Charlevoix. We sold our house on Park Avenue and moved into my present home on Michigan Ave. In 1968, we invited my mother Ethel to move to Charlevoix for company. During the long winters, I continued my writing, which was beginning to blossom.

Things perked up in the winters, when the tennis club was built in Harbor Springs! Life became really interesting when the Crooked Tree Arts Center was started and I devoted all my time along with Jack Perry, Sally Clark, Eddi Offield,

31 Arden Park, Detroit, Michigan

510 Michigan Avenue, Charlevoix, Michigan

Caroline Rader, Marilyn Davies, Ima Williams, Barbara Burt, Joan MacGillivray, Melissa Keiswetter and other good friends to help promote this worthwhile project.

During the summers the house was filled with a steady stream of family from both coasts, Patsy and Jay from the east and Margot from the west. My three nephews, Walter, Peter and Larry, took turns, each spending a year with us while attending Charlevoix High School. Their presence was a great pleasure for both of us.

Nate and Joanne Cummings bought the Anchorage on Lake Charlevoix during the '60's. We all became close friends. Joanne and I played tennis in the summer and skied together in the winter

1984 was a very bad year! My beloved husband died the day after our 45th anniversary. My mother passed away a month later. It took about a year to recover from these two difficult losses before I was able to throw myself again into the joy of volunteer work and writing.

Fortunately my desire for travel could be once again realized. Alyce Lesser and I went on a wonderful trip to Florence and Paris with a group of her friends from St. Louis. In 1986 my friend Doris Lundteigen invited me to join her on a nostalgic trip to Shanghai, which included a side trip to Beijing and a trip down the Yellow River. In 1993 I went by myself to see the magnificent Royal Tables of Europe at the Palace of Versailles, and with luck was taken on a private tour by the curator throughout the Palace, a thrilling experience!

Several years later, I attended a fabulous wedding in a *domo* on a canal in Venice with my friend Gertrude Kasle. The day before leaving for Vienna, I broke my leg and was

Her Crooked Tree Arts Council Honor

Edith Sets the Table

Edith Gilbert, Author

Summer Resort Life: Tango, Teas and All, Jet'iquette, 1995
The Complete Wedding Planner, Warner Books, 1983
Tabletops, The Right Way. Jet'Iquette, 1980
Let's Set the Table, Jet'Iquette, 1973
All About Parties, Heartwind Publications,1968

laid up in an Italian hospital for a month where no one spoke a word of English! But I did get good care from Gail Wiemer and Carolina Smith who came to Italy to help. I finally flew home via Detroit, where my dear friends, the Keiswetters, had a driver transport me to Charlevoix in a car where I could lie down and stretch out! Such a blessing!

Now that my travel days are over, Up North is the place to be and there is no other place I would rather live! Delightful people have settled here year 'round. There are wonderful restaurants to choose from as well as concerts, plays, foreign films and art exhibits to attend with friends and neighbors. Even the hard winter climate has mellowed.

Fortunately Jay and Vicky Gilbert and their lovely children Curtis, Vicci, and Jennifer all honor me with their presence during the year. Margot and her children Janet, Peter and Larry are frequent summer visitors. And now another generation, Claire, Jake, Helen, Carl, Jay, Olivia and Jack are also enjoying the tennis court, golfing and the beach.

The Beverly Hills Hotel

Margot & Ethel at a Garden Party

Margot and Edith, 1938

Growing Up In Beverly Hills
Margot W. Smith

In 1936, my family moved from San Francisco into a flat at 228 Rexford Drive in Beverly Hills. I was six years old. It was during the midst of the Great Depression and my father was unemployed. However, shortly after we arrived, my mother was invited to open a shop in the Beverly Hills Hotel by its manager, Hernando Courtright. At the time the hotel was bankrupt and owned by the Bank of America. Her store was in the lobby just to the left of the front door and her merchandise included jewelry, Chinese imports, china. Ethel Wiesinger, Gifts had a stand for magazines, newspapers, comic books, candy and cigarettes. She had the store from 1936 to 1949.

Her main customers were wealthy widows who lived at the hotel and came down every afternoon at four for tea in the leather-furnished Persian-carpeted lobby. Among them was Mrs. Astaire, Fred Astaire's mother, Mrs. Hetherington, and Mrs. Huntington. I remember taking tea with them, snitching *hors d'oeuvres* at weddings, and getting swimming lessons in the hotel pool. I read all the comic books at mother's shop; they came in every month.

I liked to visit with Vally Wieselthier, a Viennese artist who worked outdoors on one of the hotel balconies. She was nice to me, offering this eight or nine year old child cookies. One day I saw her sculpting a hippopotamus

Margot on her Bike, Pegasus

dressed in a tutu lying on a chaise longue, a sculpture about 10 inches high, and she commented that she was sending it to Walt Disney. I admired it and ran off, never dreaming that I would see her hippo in the movie, *FANTASIA,* the dance of the hippopotamuses.

I hung out in the hotel upholstery shop, where the lady upholsterers were good to me. At that time, the hotel refurbished its own rooms and had its own upholstery staff. Since watching them for hours, I've always known how to upholster.

Because of the shop in the Beverly Hills Hotel, I was sent to kindergarten at nearby Hawthorne School. One day my father was late picking me up and I decided to walk to the Hotel. I had to cross Sunset Boulevard, not heavily trafficked in those days, and there was a bridle path for horses down the middle. I didn't know the difference between bridle and bridal, and wondered about the weddings that took place there, the bride walking down the dusty path--to where? This five year old's walk to the hotel created a great furor, and I ended up going to Beverly Vista Elementary School across the street from our flat on Rexford Drive where I attended first to eighth grade.

We lived in the downstairs flat; upstairs was another family and the landlord lived in an apartment over the garage in the back. Many were immigrants— my mother was from Austria, the family upstairs were French, the landlord was Lithuanian; one best friend's father was from Norway and another's parents were from Poland.

We children played outside; we all knew kick-the-can, tag, jump rope, jacks, hop scotch, hide-and-seek. Two houses away was an empty lot that grew tall weeds where we played in its jungle, building clubhouses out of corrugated boxes. We rode our bikes and skated everywhere. I hung out at the public library and read, read, read. We came home when the sun set and listened to the radio—*The Lone Ranger, The Shadow, I Love a Mystery.*

Our neighborhood was served daily by the Arden milkman who left milk in glass bottles on our doorstep and picked up the empties every morning. In the afternoon, the Helms Bakery van stopped with bread and sweets. In the summer the ice cream truck came by playing music and we would run to buy popsicles. In the back of the house was an alley for the garbage truck, and in these days before smog, every house had an incinerator to burn combustible trash.

My father drove his old Buick home every evening, but often it was out of gas, so in the morning, our job was to help push the car up to the Richfield Gas Station on the corner so he could buy a few cents worth for the day. Unfortunately, he was not successful in finding work and eventually left for New York and Europe.

Living across the street from school was fun; we used the playground. I was not a very good student. I had learned to read at age three; when the class would be reading *See Jane Run* I would look ahead to see how it came out. When the teacher called on me, I would be in the wrong place. Eighth grade math was a bore, we only added, subtracted, multiplied and divided bigger and bigger numbers. But we had art classes with painting and pottery, music where we sang Bach, and for a very short time in the 4th grade I played the violin in the school orchestra. Civics was wonderful, our teacher taught us the Constitution line and verse; I learned my rights. Years later, I learned that I was an average student in the fast track.

At that time, Beverly Hills electricity was 50 megahertz while the rest of the world used 60 megahertz. What this meant was that appliances were designed especially for us. My mother once gave me a record player that used 60 megahertz so I listened to my records at a very slow speed. I think this changed after the war. It's a wonder that I learned to appreciate music.

Sometimes my mother took me with her to visit friends. Mother took me at age 12 to a party that stands out in my memory: the unveiling of a portrait by Salvador Dali of Mrs. Welz, a Jewish refugee from Holland who lived in a house across the street from the Beverly Hills Hotel.

Isabel Tas Welz by Salvador Dali

Now at the State National Gallery, Berlin

Occasionally mother took special Asian artwork to a Mr. Burkhardt who lived in a mansion in Bel Aire. He had a wonderful collection of antiques and art, including a Rubens, which I loved.

On December 7, 1941 this 12 year old joined a group of adults gathered by the Philco radio in the lobby of the Hotel to and hear our president, FDR, announce that the Japanese had bombed Pearl Harbor. It was December 7th, a day of infamy.

Everything changed. The Hotel became a center for Hollywood stars, Liz Taylor's father Howard had an art gallery downstairs, and other celebrities came to the Hotel for events, and mother knew many of them—Herbert Marshall, Walt Disney, Carmen Miranda among them.

And our lives changed. I grew a Victory Garden in the back yard. We were issued Ration Books for food and gasoline. Helms Bakery no longer had gas or tires to deliver door to door. The milkman drove a truck on its rims, very noisy, as no tires were available. We saved aluminum foil, rubber bands, fat, and the lead tubes that held toothpaste for the war effort. We bought saving stamps and bonds. And mother welcomed Jewish refugees to our home who told us of the atrocities they had suffered.

She also maintained contact with her Japanese friends, storing some of their furniture while they were in camps, that she returned to them after the war. Some made artificial flowers in the camps which mother tried to sell. After the war, she allowed a returned craftsman to share her shop, where he repaired china.

Mr. Williams Science Class, 1945

One problem that I did not realize at the time was that at Beverly Hills High School, from 1944-1948 when I was there, all our textbooks had been printed before 1942 as there was a wartime paper shortage. This did not make much difference in history or English, but our physics and chemistry classes suffered. In 1960, I was shocked to go into a physics lab at the university and see the Periodic Table all filled in.

On August 15, 1945, my friend Nancy and I rode a streetcar down Hollywood Boulevard to celebrate the war's end. The street was full of celebration, music, overjoyed crowds. In 1946, my mother was able to buy one of the first cars produced after the war, a Ford, and I learned to drive. In 1948, I graduated from High School and went on to USC, UCLA , the University of Hawaii and UC Berkeley.

Those years in Beverly Hills were special, clearly the city has changed a lot since then. I value the education I was given, at a time when California's public schools ranked among the best in the nation. *Published: Beverly Hills High School, Alumni Newsletter, April 2020*

Margot's 80th Birthday

Margot with Grandchildren
Chris, Claire, Alex, Helen and Carl
2010

Claire and Jake Linney, Janet's Children
With Bella and Jay, Jake's Children

Margot's Life: My Family Story
Margot W. Smith

I was born in San Francisco in 1930 at the beginning of the Great Depression when my mother was in her 40s, my father in his 50's, and my sister Edith was 13. I'm not sure I was particularly welcome, but my mother was loving and my father doted on me. We lived on Van Ness Avenue near the Presidio. Across the street was my Godmother, a sweet old lady named Wilhelmina Kroll (Tante Minnie; she had a lot of sorrows). One of my middle names is Wilhelmina, which I didn't know until I saw my hospital birth certificate as an adult.

According to my mother, my infant name was The Empress of China. For some reason I never felt warmly received by Mother's relatives, perhaps because when I was born, a cousin was dying in the same hospital and relatives were visiting both the cousin and my mother. (At that time women stayed in the hospital for two weeks.) Or because I was the product of a mixed marriage, Jewish and Christian?

Sunday afternoon we went for drives in the country with my mother and father down the San Francisco Peninsula to visit friends. We had a large Buick touring car. We would ride for an hour or so and I would be car sick. Mother thought I could be cured of carsickness and drove me around the block for hours when I was a baby.

We often attended festivities at the San Francisco *Schlaraffia (Utopia)*, a German fraternity that was always festive with German music, food and my father

Margot Rosaly Wiesinger

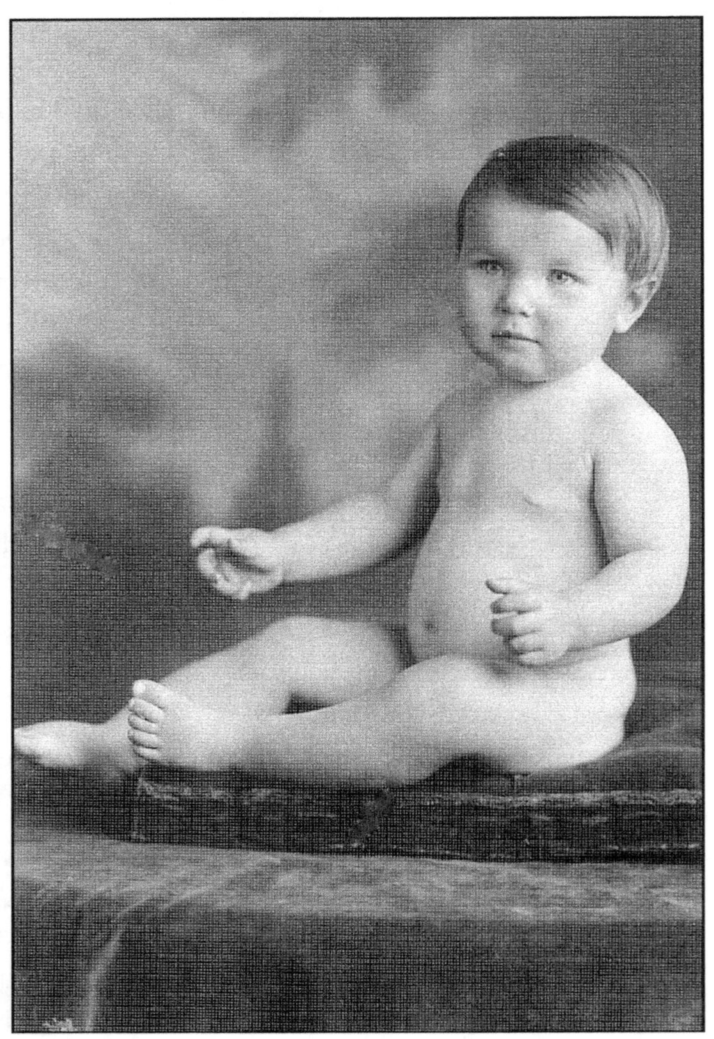

Born August, 1930

reading poetry that he composed. Later we went to Oktoberfests in Los Angeles at Hindenberg Park, (named after the prime minister of Germany) where they danced the Schuhplattler and played the accordion.

My parents had an Asian arts store in the St. Francis Hotel in San Francisco that went bankrupt in 1934, partly because of the Depression and partly because of their pro-Hitler leanings. It was a time of political upheaval. Hitler was coming to power and dividing the German community; Mussolini was coming to power and dividing the Italian community. The Schlaraffia was politically split. Mother always said that they did not believe what they heard was happening in Germany during this time because there had been so many lies and propaganda about German atrocities during World War I.

In 1934, while Otto stayed in San Francisco to finish the bankruptcy proceedings, mother took trunks of merchandise to hotels in Los Angeles, Beverly Hills and Santa Barbara, to sell fine arts at trunk shows and send money to the family as she was able. During the months she was away, Edith and I, my father and a maid stayed in San Francisco where I celebrated my fourth birthday.

This was a painful experience for mother; she wrote "I am alone, a stranger in a strange land." A letter at the time noted that I insisted on being called Judith as it went better with Edith; it also noted that she thought I was celebrating my fifth birthday when I was four. Mother did not like to talk about this time.

Edith and Margot

San Francisco, 1930

Moving South

Still in financial straits, we moved to Hollywood in 1935 and lived in a little wooden house on Palm Drive. A five year old, I was continually being told to get out from underfoot. By then I knew how to read. The kids in the neighborhood teased me a lot. My parents fought constantly. One night I heard a door slam and panicked, I thought my father had left the house and went running after him, but it turned out that he had not. I was chasing a strange man.

I attended a nursery school that I liked. It was a large place, perhaps 50 children. We had a play yard and I had a special friend, Peter. At lunch we sat at four long rows of tables with about 25 children on each side of each table. I'm sure they were hurting for money; they served us milk toast with applesauce and cinnamon for lunch. (Milk toast was toasted bread soaked in warm milk with sugar and butter.) My father combed my hair and got me ready for school each day. He smelled of cigars. I was happy at nursery school.

Sometime during this period while father was unemployed mother opened a shop in a little English cottage-like store on Sunset Boulevard, a venture that only lasted a few months. She was then invited to open a store in the Beverly Hills Hotel, which at the time was bankrupt and under the management of the Bank of America.

At the Beverly Hills Hotel her main customers were old ladies who lived at the hotel. Every afternoon at four o'clock they came down for tea in the leather-

Margot at Age Three

San Francisco, 1933

furnished Persian-carpeted lobby and were served tea from a silver service into china cups. Among the hotel residents were Ann Astaire, Fred's mother, Mrs. Hetherington and other wealthy women. mother was charming and catered to them and they supported her by buying at the gift shop. I had cookies with them and snitched *hors d'oeuvres* at weddings and had swimming lessons in the hotel pool.

As an adult, I met a woman who was a judge in Los Angeles. She recalled that when she was brought to California as a child by her mother, who wanted her to become a movie star. She took her to meet mother at the Beverly Hills Hotel, probably thinking that she had connections. There were many famous child stars at the time: Shirley Temple, Jane Withers, Margaret O'Brian, Elizabeth Taylor, Roddy McDowell. The desire to become a child star was not uncommon.

At mother's shop I read all the comic books that came in every month and climbed the back passages to the hotel towers where there was an artist working. I wandered the hotel and knew every nook and cranny. Downstairs in the Arcade, Howard Taylor (Elizabeth Taylor's father) owned an art gallery, and I remember the excitement when we all ran there to see a stunning oil painting by Angelica Kauffman (1740-1807). Stella de Malzeville had a photography studio there where she shot glamorous portraits of guests and movie stars.

There was also a barbershop at the lower level and an upholstery shop where women re-upholstered hotel furniture. They were kind to me and I spent many hours watching them work, and as a result have always

The Bridle Path, Sunset Boulevard

The Beverly Hills Hotel Lobby, 1936

known how to upholster. I never was allowed into the famous Polo Room where they served cocktails, but I learned to swim in the hotel pool and spent many hours there.

Soon after mother opened the shop we moved from Hollywood to 228 Rexford Drive in Beverly Hills. Because she had her shop in the Beverly Hills Hotel, I was sent to kindergarten at nearby Hawthorne School. One day my father was late picking me up so I walked the several blocks to the hotel by myself. My walk to the hotel alone at age five created a great furor and I ended up going to Beverly Vista School across the street from our flat on Rexford Drive

I was much happier on Rexford Drive. We lived across from the schoolyard and there were neighbor kids who were my friends. Next door was the Wright family. The father taught at the high school and they had four children; Lorraine and Freddy were my friends. They were my first exposure to a family where the parents expressed affection for each other and the children were natural: rambunctious, outgoing, playful.

Many immigrants made their home in our area. Down the block lived Nancy Norman and her mother, father and brother; her father was from Norway. Her parents owned a tiny restaurant that served home cooking over a counter, like a take out. Nancy and I were best friends but at age 13 she went to school out of the district. We have stayed in touch and are lifelong friends.

Upstairs in our building was a family from France. In the rear of our flat was an apartment over the garage

Ethel, Margot, Otto and Edith

This is the only photo of us together, 1935

Nancy Norman and Margot Wiesinger, 1944.

where our landlord, the Smardak family, lived. They were from Lithuania and had two daughters, Christine and Louise. They were about eight years older than I, but enjoyed playing trading cards. *(Trading cards were playing cards with pictures on them. They were traded like baseball cards).*

My parents and their friends were constantly talking politics, Germany, Hamburg, Hitler. When I was about six I wrote a garbled narrative of what I was hearing in a booklet. One day my parents found it and were horrified. They destroyed it.

Father was not successful at finding employment; he was in his 50s and it was the depths of the Depression. For a short time he moved to Carmel, California and opened a shop in a Tudor style cottage on the main street. However, this failed. As mother took the lead in the business there was now a power struggle. She did not care about bookkeeping and he was meticulous. She took money out of the cash drawer as needed; this enraged him.

When I was six, my father left for New York and Germany, and I did not see him again until I was 24. After he left, he wrote me many letters, but I dreaded the letters; they were always full of advice irrelevant to my life.

Mother was very social, both at the hotel and personally. At times, she took me to visit her friends. Some were her best customers and some were Asia Society or Schlaraffia connections. Some were old German people in very quiet houses. (The Stones, the Koretz, the Weills, Mr. Burkhardt, and more.) I was shocked when the Stones committed suicide together when I was about 10. The

Koretz's were wealthy; they owned a clothing company and lived in a mansion in Bel Air. We visited them and I swam in their pool. One time they invited me and some of my friends to swim and blow up balloons for an elegant party. Other friends of mother were the Weill's who had a son who was a famous Broadway producer. (Kurt Weill) Many were refugees from Hitler's Germany.

My sister Edith, 13 years older than I, was a popular, social creature at Galileo High School in San Francisco. When we moved to Beverly Hills it was traumatic; all of a sudden she was a nobody. She never forgave mother for depriving her of her senior year with her friends at Galileo High. Moreover, in our new home she was supposed to come home after school and look after for me. She rarely did. She went to the Beverly Hills Hotel swimming pool and tennis courts for the social life. Once after elementary school I came home and cooked up scrambled eggs for my friends and generally made a huge mess with the neighborhood kids in the house running wild. This did not go over well.

In 1938 mother hired a housekeeper, Tante Martha *(Aunt Martha)*, who said she had been a governess for the Rockefellers in her youth. Her maiden name was Martha Schaaf and she married an agriculturalist named Matenaers from Germany who introduced cotton to the San Joaquin valley. He died suddenly during the Depression leaving her penniless. So she came to work for mother.

I, to this day, do not understand how she could have been a governess. Although she was fond of me she gave me absolutely no training or instruction of any sort but acted more as a maid, cook, house cleaner. Moreover, she was depressed in her later years. When I came home from school she would complain that she would like to stick her head in the oven and die. She later appealed to the Rockefellers for a pension that they granted so she could retire.

My experience growing up in the store was dullsville. The store was full of elegant Asian imports, ivory, jewelry, china, silk, and silver. Although I appreciated their beauty, I don't recall learning of their history or origins. The tasks mother gave me were dusting, sweeping, gift wrapping; nothing that required knowledge of art or antiques. I was supposed to observe and obey, traits that do not come to me naturally.

Unlike mother and Edith who cultivated relationships with the hotel guests and the Hollywood stars, the people I got to know well were the shop's sales women. Many were marginally affiliated with the movie industry, Mario Lanza's sister-in-law, a producer's widow, etc. They worked out of necessity and were usually very down to earth. One of their daughters, Dolores Hart, became a starlet and later a nun. Often they would move on or mother would discharge them for one reason or another, so these relationships were not long lasting.

Mother's Family

Mother was from Chernowitz in the Bukovina, a part of the Austro-Hungarian Empire, now Ukraine.

Ethel, Margot and Tante Martha

228 Rexford Drive, Beverly Hills, California

German was spoken in the schools, and mother learned German, French and English as part of her schooling.

She was the last of eleven children and said that no one paid attention to her. Her father often offered her a pfennig (penny) if only she would stop talking. Of the eleven children, only six grew to adulthood as some were lost to childhood diseases. Once when her father left home with teams of horses to haul schnapps in wagons from Czernowitz to Bosnia-Herzegovina; on his return he found that four babies had died from diphtheria.

The siblings that mother knew were Joseph, Dora, Lulu (Lily), Regina, and Ben. Joseph came to America and disappeared. They never found out what happened to him. Dora married and moved to Shanghai where mother and her parents visited when they left Austria. They thought that she had married a diplomat, but he was not; he had lied and really just ran a small hotel. Dora died from Brights disease at a relatively young age. Lulu also was in China and died at the age of 28.

Regina went from Chernowitz to New York to marry a distant relative, Otto Goldberg. She had four children, Albert, Jules, Nathan and Marian, and died as a young woman from appendicitis.

Among the relatives I knew were mother's brother Ben Liebman and his wife Jeanette, their son Perry and his first wife Isabel, their children Jean and Brad, and Jeanette's sister Kate. They lived in San Francisco.

According to mother, Ben and Jeanette were going together before the 1906 earthquake and broke up, but they found each other after the quake and married

Ruth, Jules and Carolyn Gilbert
(Goldberg)

Cousins from New York, 1938

soon afterwards. Ben was in construction. They built many houses in San Francisco after the quake, much of the Marina district. Mother said he never was good in school and Jeanette did all the bookwork. He died in 1948 at the age of 64. Jeanette lived to be 84 and died as the result of a fall. Mother commented when she died "She died so soon, she came from such a long lived family!" In fact, Jeanette's mother died when Jeanette was quite young from an illegal abortion and Jeanette was apprenticed at an early age as a milliner (hat maker). When I knew her, she loved to travel, was heavily into drink and had a sharp tongue. She was famous for saying she brushed her teeth with scotch.

Regina's son Jules, his wife Ruth and daughter Carolyn moved to Los Angeles in the 1930's and visited regularly. I was particularly fond of Jules. Ruth was the driving force in the family. She was from the Bronx, and an avid bridge player.

Because of discrimination against Jews, Jules changed his name from Goldberg to Farrar (Ruth's maiden name) and then to Gilbert. His brother Nathan changed his name to Colbert. Only Albert remained a Goldberg. His sister Marian's husband, because of discrimination against Italians, changed his name from Piccirilli to Pick. Mother was furious with Jules for changing his name to Gilbert because Jules Gilbert was very similar to Edith's husband's name, Julius Gilbert.

All this name changing led me later to write a paper on the prevalence of name-changing and why it happens and doesn't happen. Some cultures value family names and others, like Jewish families, do not. In our German family, if I had been a boy and could have carried on the Wiesinger name my life might have been very different. *(See Margot Smith, **What's in a Name? When Names Change,** Researchgate.com)*

Jules, Ruth and daughter Carolyn moved from New York to Los Angeles during the height of the 1930s Depression. They were very poor. At first he sold Fuller Brush household deodorizer door to door. When mother had them over for dinner on Sundays they walked from their apartment in Hollywood to Beverly Hills to save the carfare. Later, he became a plumber, then a contractor, then a developer of housing tracts in the San Fernando Valley. His pièce de résistance was an eight story medical building in Encino built long before there was thought of development in the area. The family ended up very well off, thanks to his industry and Ruth's business acumen.

Carolyn adored horses, and married several times, first to a Hollywood stunt man, by whom she had a son, Shane. Her second husband was a rancher, and she had another son, Chad. Her third husband was also a rancher. She lived on their ranch near Hollister. I became better acquainted with her when I was doing research on my doctoral dissertation on rural health care in Hollister, CA in the mid 1970's. She died at age 62.

Mother went to New York now and then to visit her other relatives but I never met them. I was much younger than my cousins. I was the age of their children.

Margot, Ben, Patsy, Frankie and Jay

Charlevoix, 1942

Summers in Charlevoix

My sister Edith married Julius Gilbert in 1940, moved to Detroit and summered in Charlevoix, Michigan. For years I went to Charlevoix for vacations. My first trip there was in 1941 when Mother, Aunt Jeanette and I traveled by train across the country on the *Super Chief* in our own compartment.

The following year at age 12 I went by train alone. I stayed at the elegant Palmer House Hotel in Chicago overnight, thanks to Mother's connections with the manager of the Beverly Hills Hotel. I arrived late and so to feed me I was taken to the nightclub at the hotel and saw the jazz pianist Eddie Duchin 's show; it was his last before going off to war.

The First Visit to Charlevoix

Jeanette, Ethel, Edith, Sylvia and Nana, 1941

210 Park Avenue, Charlevoix, Michigan

The next evening I was put on the Pere Marquette train to Charlevoix, an overnighter that ran regularly from Chicago to accommodate the wealthy families with summer homes who stayed in cool northern Michigan during the Midwest's hottest months, before air conditioning was invented. Later I was sent to Charlevoix by plane, a DC3, flying from Los Angeles and making stops in Amarillo, Texas, and St. Louis, Missouri, before landing in Chicago.

When Edith and Julius first married, they lived with his parents at 31 Arden Park, Detroit where the Gilbert household included Edith and Julius, Julius' father, Sam, his mother Sylvia and grandmother Nana. In the summer, all went to Charlevoix to enjoy the cooler weather. There, Patsy and Jay, Julius' children by his first marriage, and I, Edith's young sister, were added to the mix. The Gilberts had a large house on Park Avenue. Later Julius and Edith bought another house across the street.

The family's wealth was due to the acumen of Julius' father, Sam "S.T." Gilbert, who ran the R. G. Dun Cigar Company, a well-known brand. This later became the DWG Company, Diesel-Wemmer-Gilbert. I toured the factory once when I was in Detroit and saw R. G. Dun Cigars being rolled by hand. The smell of raw tobacco where people worked was overwhelming. Julius' income was from the stock market. As far as I know, he was never employed.

In Charlevoix, I was sent to camp with other kids; I went horseback riding and sailed on the Sylvia G II, Pat-E-Jay and other Gilbert boats. At first, Patsy and Jay were there. Jay was a sweet boy who enjoyed fishing and boating with his father. However, Patsy was a troubled child; one year they had a psychiatric social worker living in the house to help care for her. After she attacked me once, Patsy and I were not hosted in Charlevoix at the same time. I did not see her again until years later.

The Gilbert home on Park Avenue had an upstairs maid, downstairs maid, cook and chauffeur and were housed in servants quarters in the attic and over the garage. They were immigrants from Poland and Czechoslovakia and were brought from Detroit for the summer. Loren Johnson, the chauffeur and boat captain, lived with his Finnish wife and two sons over the garage. He was a WWI veteran who had been gassed during the war and suffered health consequences. Frankie, Loren's son and Jay were best friends.

After World War II, this all changed. The live-in servants aged and retired and were not replaced. By 1948, Sam, Sylvia and Nana were deceased. Julius and Edith then moved to a modern elegant home at 510 Michigan Avenue. In 1962, they left Detroit and moved to Charlevoix permanently.

Charlevoix summers were in sharp contrast to my life at home in Beverly Hills. Charlevoix was a resort for the wealthy; home was a middle-class shopkeepers existence. I had trouble relating to the children of the rich. Once I joined them in a poker game and lost $3 in 15 minutes and realized this was not for me.

The War Years

During World War II mother knew many Jewish refugees who were escaping Nazi persecution. She was part of an international community and housed escapees entering the US legally and illegally. From when I was about age 10 and on, they would visit and tell of the horrors they experienced in Germany. One older man showed me how he could move his thumb knuckle to look like a man chewing; the nail had been removed. I recall to this day not being entertained but horrified. Another visitor was a woman named Mrs. Greiner; she was about six feet tall and had been smuggled across the Mexican border curled up hidden in half a car's gas tank.

While mother aided many refugees from Hitler, at times, when she was with other German friends, she took part in their activities. Once she danced around the piano with them when Germany invaded Norway. Later, she felt unfairly, she was put on the FBI black list because she showed merchandise to Nazi filmmaker Leni Riefenstahl in her Beverly Hills Hotel room while she was a guest there. Czernowitz, her birthplace, was at times occupied by either Allied or Axis countries: the USSR, Germany, Poland, and Romania. As a result she could not get citizenship until after the war.

Many war refugees attended Beverly Hills High School. They were the children of Jews and others from Germany, Italy, France and England. Two sisters of Dutch ancestry in my art class had been in Japanese concentration camps in Malaysia during the war and were in school to finish high school. I'll never forget their paintings full of pain and trauma.

Hamburg, 1954

Margot & Walter's Passport Photo

Edith, Walter and Otto

There was much anti-German feeling during the war and mother was reluctant to speak German in public. I had no inclination to learn German at school. During World War II, all mail was cut off from Germany; we could not hear from my father for those years. When the war ended in 1945 an American soldier forwarded a letter from him and we found he had survived and was living in Berlin.

In 1948 and 1949, the USSR blockaded West Berlin from all incoming transport and the American Sector depended on an American Air Lift for supplies to be flown in. Mother and Edith helped Otto in this dire strait by sending him the food that he liked and needed and nylon stockings to sell on the Black Market. He reciprocated by sending Mother fine china for her to sell. I still have a set of his Rosenthal demitasses.

When the blockade ended, he moved to Hamburg and worked as a translator. After the war in 1954, Edith, my one-year-old son Walter and I went to visit him and

Rosenthal Demitasse Set

his wife Gertrude. It was not a very satisfactory visit; I did not know him very well and he did not seem interested in me or in his grandson.

Later, on our return, Edith and I realized that we had not met one neighbor, colleague, friend or any other person the whole time we were in Hamburg. We could only conclude our father did not want anyone there to meet his half-Jewish American daughters.

Mother had many Japanese connections. She imported Japanese silk yardage and after cutting it into segments on the kitchen table she took them to her Japanese seamstress to sew into beautiful kimonos that she sold in the store. When the Japanese were sent to internment camps during the war, she stored furniture for them and kept in contact. After the war, she returned the furniture and allowed Yoshi, a china repairer, to share her shop until he could get on his feet. I still have some china he repaired. He was very uncommunicative; to this day I do not know if he spoke English or if he was silent because of shock from his experience.

Yoshi's Space

Off to College

Although an avid reader, I was never a particularly good student, getting B's and C's throughout school, but somehow I always knew that I must go to college. As a high school senior I had to figure out how to apply, how to take entrance exams, where to go. Mother was completely clueless. Furthermore, my father wrote her "Why should she go to college? She will only get married,."

I don't remember being informed about Merit Exams or scholarships but somehow I discovered how to take college entrance exams, took them and was in the 90th percentile for everything except math. Curiously, although I got a B in senior high school English, I qualified for advanced placement in college freshman English. When I showed this to my English teacher, Miss Schmidt, she said "Oh I don't think you should do that." Naturally I ignored her advice.

Mother had saved money for my college, but was persuaded by a realtor to invest this money in Desert Hot Springs acreage. When we visited the vast mesquite covered sand, he pointed to a hill far away and said "Janet Gaynor has a ranch there." Janet Gaynor was a famous movie star. Naturally, this impressed Mother so she bought 10 acres, dreaming of founding a women's colony there. So there went my college fund.

I inherited the land in 1984 and paid taxes on it until 1998 when I sold it for $10,000. As one realtor put it, it was "outside the sphere of development." Selling it was an adventure. I researched selling it over the years.

Margot, the High School Graduate

Desert Hot Springs Land, 1998

*Margot Plants
St. Joseph Upside Down to Sell the
Acreage*

Since the area was famous for its hot springs I could soak and get a massage while visiting. Finally, in 1998 I heard that if one planted a statue of St. Joseph the Worker upside down on a property, it would help sell it. So one day my friend Shirley Harlan and I stopped by and buried St Joseph upside down on the property and sprinkled him with a little gin. I then put an ad in the Desert Hot Springs newspaper and shortly got an offer, curiously by a man named Luther. It finally sold to another dreamer.

In 1948, I entered the University of Southern California with the help of Edith's financing. Edith had decided that I should be an occupational therapist. At USC I took one OT class and hated it. I preferred sociology. At the time, 1948-1950, a majority of USC students were World War II veterans going to school on the GI Bill. There were about 10 men to every woman. I was absolutely clueless as to socializing. I had never dated but eventually caught on. While looking for ways to make social contacts, I saw that sororities were seeking members and I naively signed up, stating my mother's religion. During their rush I invited mother to a mother-daughter tea and I saw how these tall Anglo-Saxon women viewed her, a tiny Jewish woman with a foreign accent. That was the end of that.

I met my future husband at USC. When I became engaged, Edith and mother did not like my choice and refused to continue to pay tuition at USC, so I transferred to UCLA. The last semester at UCLA I became ill and had to drop several classes so I could not graduate. This debacle meant that I finally finished my bachelor's degree in 1965 at the University of Hawaii at the age of 35.

UCLA was another world. As a bookish nerd, I was fascinated with the library. I listened to recordings of music that Alan and John Lomax had collected in the South. Folk music was just coming into consciousness. My high school friend Marcia Furstenberg (later Scott) introduced me to folk music; I'm forever grateful. I adored Josh White, Burl Ives, Woody Guthrie, Lead Belly, Richard Dyer-Bennet, Jean Ritchie. Guy Carawan had hootenannies nearby. Even I played the guitar and sang. But then, the commercial Kingston Trio came along and ruined amateur folk song for us. Marcia and I were lifelong friends; she became a psychiatrist in Boston.

I felt the need to help earn my keep so I got a job with the Church Federation of Los Angeles. I was sent to Watts to lead recreation groups in local churches. That was a huge eye opener. Watts then was full of tract houses with African American veterans who bought them on GI Bill hoping for more economic opportunity after WWII, but opportunities were minimal. Civic neglect and poverty was rampant. The schools were impoverished and the kids undereducated. I knew one high schooler who commuted to Hollywood High School two hours away because she wanted a proper education.

I had a wonderful supervisor, Vida Van Brunt, who tried to educate me. We became life long friends. She told me that the first place that burned during the Watts rebellion in 1965 was a furniture store that repossessed family furniture after only one missed payment.

Another Church Federation site where I worked was in East Los Angeles, Happy Valley, among Mexican American kids. Same story.

Leaving Home

I married in 1952, and moved to Salinas and then Norwalk, California. From 1953 to 1959, I had four children, Walter, Janet, Peter and Larry. While living in our GI Bill tract home in Norwalk, Mother visited often and enjoyed her grandchildren. In 1959, we moved to Hilo, Hawaii where visiting was more difficult and expensive.

Grandma Ethel Plays Ring Around the Rosy

Living in Hawaii was wonderful: the tropical flowers, the weather, the aloha spirit. In 1960 we experienced the power of the ocean when a 20 foot tidal wave washed through the downtown and demolished it. We housed a couple of families, helping when we could.

Walter, Peter, Margot, Larry, Janet and Ethel
A Visit to Grandma Ethel in Hollywood, 1966

University of California, Berkeley
Graduation, 1977

Ethel, Margot, Peter and Janet

In 1964, after divorcing, the children and I moved to Honolulu. I resumed my education at the University of Hawaii finishing a Bachelors in Education and Masters in American Studies. Mother had retired by then, and since it seemed unlikely that I would return to Beverly Hills; in 1967 she moved to Charlevoix to be near my sister. Edith bought a house near hers where Mother lived until she died in 1984. Mother enjoyed Charlevoix life and had many friends. We visited many times. She enjoyed being a grandmother; my children spent much time in Charlevoix so they knew her well.

In 1969 the kids and I moved from Honolulu to Berkeley, California. After working a few years in research for the State of California I entered graduate school and completed a Doctorate in Public Health Social Sciences at the University of California, Berkeley in 1977. I was pleased that mother could be at graduation. I then worked in health care research and retired in 1999.

Mother dictated her life's story in 1980. Her audio tapes were used as the basis for this history of the family so that my children and grandchildren could enjoy knowing her. We were fortunate to have letters, stories and photographs with other stories that could be included.

It is a story of resilience, success in overcoming adversity and survival. She lived to the fullest; she survived a life full of challenges, political changes, wars and economic crises.

University of California Berkeley Wellness Newsletter,
April 23, 2018

Life before Vaccines
Growing up in the 1930s and 40s
Margot Smith, Dr.P.H.

Medical science has profoundly changed our lives. I am sure that I would not have survived to this old age without antibiotics, advances in epidemiology and surgery

I was a child in the 1930s. We lived in Southern California in a flat across the street from my grammar school playground and I had friends in the neighborhood. It was a time when parents simply said "Go out and play" and we did. Our games were hopscotch, kick the can, jacks, tag, jump rope, handball and hide-and-seek. We cruised on roller skates and bikes, and built club houses out of boxes in vacant lots. We were supposed to come home at twilight, before dark. The milkman, bakery truck and iceman delivered to our doors. We felt safe in our neighborhoods.

But my parents were fearful of epidemics. At school in first through 8th grades, I had classmates who suffered from scarlet fever, mumps, measles, German measles, chicken pox and whooping cough. I had rubella and had to stay in bed for several days in a darkened room; they thought light bad for sick children's eyes. Several of these diseases required the family to put a quarantine sign on their door; their children missed a lot of school.

As an adult, I knew survivors—men who could not father children because they had mumps as a child, a woman with a flail arm from polio, people with chicken pox scars, those deafened because of measles, a man who spent three years in a tuberculosis sanitarium and a woman whose child was retarded because she had German measles during her pregnancy. I have friends who had polio then who now have post-polio syndrome, that is, muscle weakness, fatigue, and pain, for which there is no known cure. They experienced their illnesses before vaccines and antibiotics.

Understanding Disease

The Discovery of Germs: In the 1930s germ theory was less than 100 years old. Although people from Biblical times knew that diseases were contagious, no one knew exactly how they were spread. In 1854 there was the famous moment when John Snow stopped an epidemic of water-borne cholera in London by removing certain water pump handles. In the 1860s, Louis Pasteur and Robert Koch found that diseases were caused by germs--this led to both a new world of medical exploration and to new fears as to how epidemics originated. We were supposed to wash our hands after we handled money because it was contaminated with germs when touched by other people.

All had heard of Typhoid Mary, the infamous cook in 1900 New York who was a typhoid carrier and infected her employers. She was finally quarantined and incarcerated. The well-known author Helen Keller was blind and deaf because of fever as a child; she was taught to communicate through sign language and later speech by her teacher, Anne Sullivan. A movie, **The Miracle Worker,** was made in 1960 about her life.

Quarantine: The discovery of germs led to the birth of the Public Health movement and laws and practices designed to control the spread of disease. At that time, the main way epidemics were prevented was by quarantine, the isolation of the ill. When I was a child patients and entire families could be quarantined. Quarantine was first used in Italy in the 14th century for ships crews coming from places with plague epidemics; later in the 19th century it was used to limit the spread of plague, cholera, yellow fever, and smallpox. Today, there are still laws for quarantining people and animals arriving on ships and planes.

These are guidelines for how long diseases are contagious and possibly how long quarantines were needed:

- Poliomyelitis: 40 days
- Diphtheria: Onset of sore throat for up to 4 weeks.
- Measles: 4 days before rash until 4 days after rash appears
- Rubella (German Measles) 7 days before rash until 5 days after rash appears
- Chicken pox: 2 days before rash until all sores have crusts (6 - 7 days)
- Scarlet fever: 21 days from the onset of the disease (in the absence of complications, 15 days)
- Mumps: 5 days before swelling until swelling gone (7 days)
- Whooping Cough: after symptoms.Onset of runny nose, 21 days
- Typhus: 12 days after the fall of temperature

The First Vaccine: People long knew that exposure to certain diseases made them immune; one could get certain illnesses only once. This was known about smallpox, which killed about 30% of those catching it and often left facial scars on survivors. In Asia, India and Turkey, it was known that inoculation with smallpox scabs could lead to a mild disease that made one immune. Lady Mary Montagu, the wife of England's ambassador to Turkey, was the first to bring the practice in the Europe. In 1715, she was disfigured as a result of smallpox. After learning about inoculation in Turkey, she was determined to protect her six-year-old son from the disease through inoculation. "The smallpox, so fatal, and so general amongst us, is [in Turkey] entirely harmless by the invention of [inoculation]," She wrote to a friend. "There is a set of old women who make it their business to perform the operation every autumn... The old woman comes with a nut-shell full of the matter of the best sort of smallpox, and asks what veins you please to have opened..."

In the 1790s, Edward Jenner, a country physician in England noticed that the faces of milkmaids, the young women who milked cows, were rarely scarred with smallpox. He found that their exposure to cowpox, an infection of cows, protected them. This led to the development of cowpox vaccination as smallpox prevention—the word vaccine is derived from the Latin, *Variolae vaccinae* (smallpox of the cow),

Immunization to smallpox was important in the Revolutionary War. George Washington in 1790 ordered mandatory inoculation for troops who hadn't survived smallpox before. However, inoculation with this live virus was dangerous: it killed about 2-3 percent of those injected with even small amounts. Today, vaccines are developed from dead or weakened bacteria or virus.

My childhood vaccination for smallpox left a scar on my upper arm, a rarity now. (Although there is an internet site which shows actresses with vaccination scars.) In the *History of Medicine in California* mural at the University of California Medical School in San Francisco, artist Bernard Zakheim shows James Ohio Pattie in 1829 vaccinating the California Alcalde (governor) with cowpox during a smallpox epidemic; vaccination was a novelty at that time and place. Massachusetts was the first state in the U.S. to require smallpox vaccination in 1902.

Now that smallpox has been eradicated, smallpox vaccinations are no longer required. The last U.S. wild smallpox case occurred in 1949 and, after extensive vaccination campaigns, the last case of smallpox in the world occurred in 1977.

Vaccines for Common Childhood Diseases

Polio: For my parents, polio was a major fear. In summer, public swimming pools were closed because of polio which thrived in summer months. The consequences of polio were serious: children lost the ability to walk, to breathe, to use a limb. Hospitals had wards full of patients living out their lives in iron lungs.

Our president, Franklin Roosevelt, was a victim of polio. He found relief from his symptoms with trips to Warm Springs, Georgia. Later, in the 1940s, polio patients were treated with exercise in warm pools, a method discovered by the Australian nurse, Sister Kenney. She invented the concept, *physical therapy*. Many cities built warm pools where children and adults with polio could find exercise.

In 1938, the *March of Dimes* was founded to fund the effort to find a vaccine. In 1946, Rosalind

Russell starred in the RKO movie, *Sister Kenney*. In 1960, 2,525 cases of paralysis due to polio were reported. In 1963, I could give my children an oral vaccine developed by Jonas Salk and Albert Sabin in a sugar cube and was grateful that I did not need to fear this dreadful disease. In 1965 there were only 61 cases in the U.S. By 1994, Polio was declared eliminated from the Americas. In 2002, it was eliminated from Europe. Today, only Pakistan and Afghanistan continue to have polio cases.

Diphtheria: In my childhood, I was not aware of anyone having diphtheria. However, my mother was from eastern Europe (Chernowitz, Ukraine), born in 1893 and the youngest of eleven children. She knew only 8 of her sibs as her parents lost 3 sons to diphtheria in one week, years before she was born. At that time, 40% of children who caught diphtheria died. The British royal family suffered from diphtheria epidemics during the late nineteenth century. Four members of the royal family died in the 1870s. Thanks to the discovery of germs as a cause of disease, diphtheria bacterium were observed by Theodor Klebs in 1883 and cultivated by Friedrich Löffler in 1884. The first successful vaccine for diphtheria was in 1923.

Vaccination for diphtheria became wildly popular in the U. S. after an outbreak in Alaska resulted in the famous *Great Race of Mercy* from the town of Nenana to Nome by dog sled. Balto, the lead sled dog on the final stretch into Nome has a statue in New York City's Central Park. The relay took five and a half days and was successful in delivering the diphtheria vaccine that saved Nome and its surrounding communities from the epidemic. The race received headline coverage in newspapers across the United States

The Race of Mercy news generated a vaccination campaign in the U.S. that dramatically reduced the incidence of the disease. In the 1920s, there were 200,000 cases of diphtheria a year in the U.S. and 15,000 deaths; there were no deaths in the U.S. in 2015. We children did not experience diphtheria because we were vaccinated. However, today, there are reports that Indonesia, Pakistan and other countries with refugees still have outbreaks and deaths.

Measles: Measles were another real danger for us children. In 1912, U.S. healthcare providers and laboratories were required to notify the health departments of measles cases. In the first ten years of reporting, there were about 6,000 measles-related deaths each year and 48,000 were hospitalized. Complications from measles were difficulty breathing, ear infections and loss of hearing, seizures, hepatitis, eye infections, and neural and heart complications. Pneumonia may be fatal.

Before 1963 when a vaccine became available, nearly all children got measles by the time they were 15 years of age. I never caught measles and was glad to vaccinate my children. We feared measles, whooping cough, rubella, mumps and scarlet fever-- they might be fatal, or make us very ill and keep us out of school for weeks. Some parents arranged to expose their children to measles and chickenpox. These diseases were far more dangerous in adults.

Preventing Childhood Diseases:

The success of small pox vaccination and the identification of specific germs led to a search for vaccines for other diseases. In my lifetime, these vaccines now protect my children and grandchildren from devastating diseases:

- 1923   diphtheria
- 1924   tetanus
- 1940   pertussis (whooping cough),
- 1961   poliomyelitis (polio),
- 1963   measles,
- 1967   mumps
- 1969   rubella (German measles)
- 1994   hepatitis B
- 1995   varicella (chickenpox)

We no longer fear epidemics and deaths from these childhood dangers because vaccination prevents them and so many people are vaccinated. These diseases are no longer commonplace. Although not all children are vaccinated, these diseases are under control.

Epidemiologists call this the **herd effect**--protection from infectious diseases that happen when most of a population is immune and protects those who are not immune. I for one am grateful that these deadly illnesses are no longer prevalent. And, if we become ill, we have antibiotics to facilitate our recovery.

Our Heroes.

As kids we loved movies that idolized those who fought disease. We all read ***The Microbe Hunters*** by Paul De Kruif (1926) which told of the wonders discovered by the scientist of our time.

In 1936, we saw ***The Story of Louis Pasteur*** showing him as a renowned scientist revolutionizing agriculture and medicine. ***The White Parade*** starring Loretta Young was a 1934 film dedicated to "the memory of Florence Nightingale." The plot concerns the travails and romances of young women as they study to become nurses.

In 1940, ***Vigil in the Night*** starred Carole

Lombard, and Brian Aherne and shows nurses working together to bring about better conditions for the care of the sick as well as fighting a smallpox epidemic.

In ***The Courageous Dr. Christian***, 1940: A doctor fights an epidemic that breaks out in the poor section of town and tries to get the rest of the town to help out. ***Angel of Mercy*** (<u>MGM</u>, 1939) is a biographical film about Clara Barton, the woman who founded the nursing profession during the Civil War.

Dr. Ehrlich's Magic Bullet (1940), is based on Dr. Paul Ehrlich's pioneer work in the chemical treatment of diseases such as TB and syphilis.

These films inspired many of us to go into the health care field, and promoted the idea that we could act to improve our own and our country's health. These were our superheroes, and except for the nurses, they did not wear capes. I look forward to further miracles in the future for my children and grandchildren.

2/24/18

The Beverly Hills Hotel, 1936

The San Francisco Marina District

*Row houses with garages
on the ground floor,
similar to Liebman Houses.
A novelty after the 1906 Earthquake.*

A Lifetime Of Dwellings
Housing in the 20th Century
Margot W. Smith

When walking through the neighborhoods of many cities, I feel that I am looking at past decades in the living present. The varieties of architecture that exist today were constructed over many decades and visually recreate an area's history. My own lifetime of dwellings began with my birth in San Francisco in 1930, childhood in Los Angeles, and as an adult in Hawaii and Berkeley, that is, mostly in California.

In contrast to the cities of Europe and the East Coast, California was built up in fairly recent times, that is, since the gold rush of 1849 and statehood in 1850. Its older architecture reflects the Spanish rule of the prior 400 years when adobe Missions and Spanish ranchos prevailed. In the 1800s, Victorians and Queen Anne homes were constructed of redwood, and in the 20th century, Hollywood bungalows, stucco Italianate, Bauhaus, Frank Lloyd Wright, Richard Neutra, Art Deco, and modern styles. Tracts of homes, Eichler houses and gated communities followed WWII, built for the returning military buying homes with GI Bill financing.

My interest in architecture partly stems from family. Several cousins were builders. My uncle Ben Liebman built houses in the Marina district of San Francisco after the 1906 earthquake. He was among the first to put a garage on the ground floor, and my mother was very proud of Liebman houses that were known to be well constructed. His son, Perry Liebman, built tract homes on the Peninsula and the multistory apartment building, Isabel Towers on Gough Street in San Francisco. Another cousin, Jules Gilbert, was among the first to build a medical center and tract homes in San Fernando Valley. So many cousins and uncles in the family were builders; somehow architecture appreciation is in my DNA.

I myself experienced many styles of California buildings. In 1936, when I was six, my mother opened a gift shop in the lobby of the Beverly Hills Hotel. At that time it was bankrupt and owned by the Bank of America. The hotel was originally designed in 1911 by Pasadena architect Elmer Grey in the Mediterranean Revival style. It had several stories and distinctive towers. She was invited to open the store by the manager, who was trying to enliven it. The hotel housed wealthy widows who were provided with housekeeping and meals, and at 4:00 in the afternoon were served tea out of a silver service in the lobby. This child would sneak cookies.

In the 1930s and 1940s, workers in Beverly Hills lived between Olympic and Pico Boulevards; the middle class between Wilshire and Olympic, and the wealthiest in the hills above Sunset Boulevard. We lived just below Wilshire Boulevard in the lower flat of a Spanish-style stucco duplex owned by the actress Irene Dunne, who differed from many in the movie industry in that she was clever about investing her earnings.

At age 10 I was sent off to boarding school for a year, Monticello School for Girls. It was housed in a

In one of many signs of the residential currents away from the aging neighborhoods lining West Adams Boulevard—only just upgraded from "Street"—the West Chester School for Girls moved into the Fitzgerald house, complete with new furnaces, in time to open for its fall 1928 semester. Renamed the Monticello School for Girls by the time it opened a year later, it would occupy 2445 for 12 more school years before moving to yet another old house in yet another declining L. A. neighborhood.

mansion on Adams Boulevard in Los Angeles and was three stories with lots of dark wood and carved furnishings, a place that had seen better days. Originally, the area had boasted mansions for the wealthy.

Our Beverly Hills High School was a two story Spanish style building right next to the 20th Century Fox movie lot where they filmed cowboy and period movies with horses and hoop skirts. I really loved looking out the windows during algebra class and seeing film- making before my eyes. Their sets were truly the Old West, wooden clapboard buildings and stagecoaches. The movie lot later became Century City. *The Bachelor and the Bobby*

Soxer with Cary Grant and Shirley Temple was filmed at Beverly High where I was an extra for a while until I was bored and wandered off.

The school was famous for its gym, which featured a swimming pool that had a basketball court that slid over it. One of the girls athletic programs was synchronized swimming, a la movie star Esther Williams. It was thought to be the gym of the future. It was also famous for being the first high school in the country to have a parking lot for student cars. At Beverly High, it mattered whether your family had a swimming pool or not—we did not

The Beverly High School Swimming Pool's Retractable Basketball Court

At 18, I went off to University of Southern California and had a part time job with Church Federation of Los Angeles. My duties were to run after-school programs in churches for children living in Watts and East Los Angeles. In Watts, my supervisor was a wonderful African American woman who introduced me to Sam Rodia, who created Watts Towers, now a national landmark. The towers are made of pottery shards he collected from wherever and created a place of beauty. He was a slightly built man whom I saw climbing over the towers as if they were a jungle gym.

Watts Towers, Los Angeles

In 1952, Watts was comprised of new GI Bill tracts of working class homes. After WWII, after President Truman desegregated under of the military, there was hope that there would be more opportunity for African Americans, many of whom had served in the military during the war. This hope was dashed by continued discrimination in jobs and housing and resulted in the Watts riots of 1965. When I worked there in 1953-54 I was shocked at the low quality of education the kids were getting, the unemployment, the poverty, and the civic neglect of the streets and public buildings. Local churches and religious leaders were strong forces in creating community under these dire conditions.

At that time, the University of Southern California was surrounded by Hollywood bungalows built in 1910-20s that, as a result of migrations during WWII, were housing African American families. Only a few Caucasian families were left; the area was a victim of white flight. As

The Carlsmith House, Hilo, Hawaii, 1960

666 Kaumana Drive, Hilo 1961

Plantation House,
2144 Lanihuli Drive, Honolulu, 1964

a student, I stayed in the dorms for a few semesters and later moved into student lodgings in one of these bungalows.

After marrying a veteran attending USC on GI Bill, we benefited from a new housing tract in Norwalk, CA, where we could buy a three bedroom, two-bath home on GI Bill for $1000 down. Every house was the same style, modern with floor to ceiling windows, but had different floor plans. We paid $10,000 for this home and over time filled it with four children. At that time, a working man could support a whole family.

Norwalk, California, 1950

Our house was at 12335 Cyclops Ave., Norwalk

From Norwalk in 1959 the family moved to Hilo, Hawaii where we first lived in a Queen Anne style mansion with a fabulous stairway into the living room, a sun porch and tower. It had a beautiful garden with ginger, heliconia, lime trees, orchids and guava. It was up two flights of stairs from the street where two giant mango trees towered over them, and where, at dawn, hundreds of magpies chattered "Where shall we go? and at sundown, "Where did you go?. What did you do?

Quonset Hut, Hawaii, A Relic of WWII

900 San Benito Road, Berkeley, 1969

1300 Shattuck Ave, Berkeley, 1984

then slept. Sadly, the Queen Anne was later torn down and the wood used for an apartment building and the garden became overgrown. We then bought a house with some art deco touches at 666 Kaumana Drive.

After my divorce in 1964, the children and I moved to Honolulu into what in Hawaii was called a plantation house. They were originally built by sugar and pineapple plantations to house workers and were stained either maroon or dark green. Plantation houses had what was quaintly called "single wall construction," which meant there was one board between the inside and outside. Of course, in the warm tropics one did not need more. The house was large so I could house my family and supplement my income by renting out parts of the basement and extra rooms upstairs to students attending the nearby University of Hawaii. When the landlady showed it to me, she proudly noted that she had wall light switches installed, rather than a string hanging down from the ceiling fixture. The rooms were finished with bagasse, sheet rock made of sugar cane stalks.

In Hawaii, many natural elements attack wooden houses--dry rot, wet rot, mold and termites among them. Our house had termites, I could put my ear to the wall and hear them chewing. Once I dropped a jug of juice on the floor of the dining room and was amazed to find that it had ended up as a puddle in the basement. After we left, the house was torn down and replaced, not surprisingly; it was in a great location and a good neighborhood near the University.

After graduating from the University of Hawaii with a Bachelors in Education, I worked as a social worker in Palolo Valley where I was surprised to find a Quonset Hut left from WWII. Built everywhere as emergency housing at one time, finding one even in the 1960's was unusual.

Returning to California in 1968, the children and I lived in a 1920s row house in the San Francisco Sunset district and later moved to a 1925 Spanish style stucco home in the Berkeley hills designed by a woman for her family. It had four bedrooms, two fireplaces and a garden, and housed me and the four children until they went off to college.

The Temple of Heaven

Stationery   **Beijing, China**

In 1995 in Beijing, China, a visit to the Temple of Heaven and the Forbidden City had special meaning for me because in the 1930s, my parents' Asian art shop had their *Temple of Heaven* stationery given to me to draw on for years. Going to the Temple of Heaven in Beijing was a special thrill.

Later, traveling, touring the Gaudi works in Barcelona, it was a real thrill to see his imaginative designs and colorful wit. Seeing Gaudi was a lifetime goal. I also had the privilege of hearing Buckminster Fuller and visiting one of his dome houses in Illinois as well as the Frank Lloyd Wright building on Maiden Lane in San Francisco and the Guggenheim Museum in New York City.

I am now living in an Italianate stucco fourplex built in Berkeley in 1924 after a devastating fire, and with luck I will be carried out of it feet first. Who would have guessed that architecture and architects would have any role in my life?

Today Berkeley is filled with new construction. Some newer places are already treasures touching on historic Spanish and Art Deco styles, while others are boring monstrosities. I hope we can both keep the beauty of our older housing and create more beauty for the present time.

APPENDICES

Liebman / Wiesinger Descendants

Ethel Liebman married Otto Wiesinger in 1916, and had two daughters: Edith Annamarie in 1917 and Margot Rosaly in 1930. Ethel and Otto were divorced in 1938. Ethel died in 1984 at the age of 94. Otto died in 1954 at the age of 74 in Hamburg, Germany.

Edith married Julius Gilbert in 1940 and moved to Detroit and Charlevoix, Michigan; Edith died in 2009 at the age of 91. Julius died in 1984. She had two stepchildren, Jay Gilbert of Rochester, NY, and Patsy Gilbert Grove, deceased.

Margot is living in Berkeley, CA; she married Jerome Smith in 1952 and had four children: Walter Arnold (1953), Janet Elizabeth (1955), Peter Jay (1956) and Laurence Chad Smith (1959). Margot and Jerry divorced in 1964. Jerry died in 2004 at the age of 77. Margot married Robert Purdy in 1978; he died in 2007 at the age of 85. He had two daughters, Maida Purdy Salinas and Laura Purdy.

Walter has two sons, Christopher Napoleon Smith (1988) and Alexander Galileo Smith (1998).

Janet and Robert Linney have a son, Jacob Thomas Linney (1984) and daughter Claire Katherine Linney (1987). Jacob Linney lives in North Carolina and has two children, Bella Elyssa (2008) and Jay Matthew (2010).

Peter and Nancy have a daughter Helen Elizabeth Smith (1989) and son Carl MacArthur Smith (1990).

Lawrence and Diane live in Michigan. *2021*

The Liebman Family

Rosa Schenker	*Meyer Liebman*
Born 1847, Zaleschiki, Galicia	*1844, Tlusta, Galicia*
Died May 23, 1933, New York City	*1920, New York City*

Buried in Montefiore Cemetery, Springfield Blvd, Queens, NY

|________________Married 1865________________|

Moved to Czemowitz, Bukovina

Liebman Offspring

(Four sons lost to diphtheria in one week)

- **Esther** (Died, age 22)

- **Dora** & Isaac Spun, (Died, age 50) Shanghai, China

- **Joseph,** Disappeared

- **Ben** & Jeanette Stein, (Died, age 64,) San Francisco, CA
    - o **Perry** & Isabel, (Died, age 72)

        Jean, Married twice, Deceased Burlingame, CA
        Children Orenstein
        Bradford & Greta, Burlingame, CA

- **Regina** & Otto Goldberg (Died, age 48) Brooklyn, NY
    - o **Nathan Colbert** & Gladys Katz
    - o **Marian &** Ray Pick**,** (Died age 75), New York
        Mary
    - o **Albert Goldberg**
    - o **Jules Gilbert** & Ruth Farrar, (Died age 72.) Encino, CA

        Carolyn, Married thrice; (Died age 62.) Hollister, CA
        Sons **Shane** and **Chad**

- **Lilly,** (Died, age 25,)

- **Ethel (**Yettie) Died, age 94,) Charlevoix, MI

    & Otto Wiesinger (Died age 74) Hamburg, Germany

    - o **Edith** & Julius Gilbert (Died age 91) Charlevoix, MI,
    - o **Margot** Smith

        Walter Smith, Loomis, CA
        Sons **Christopher and Alexander**
        Janet & Robert Linney, Watsonville, CA
        Son **Jacob,** Greensboro, NC
        Daughter **Bella** and Son **Jay**

        Daughter **Claire,**
        Peter & Nancy Smith, Clifton, VA
        Daughter **Helen** and Son **Carl,**
        Larry & Diane Smith, Pelston, MI

Ethel's Life
Timeline

1890 Born in Czernowitz, Bukovina, Austria

1910 Went to Shanghai, China with her parents

1912 Lived in New York City

1916 Married Otto Wiesinger

1917 Daughter Edith Annamarie born.

1922 Visited Hamburg, Germany

1924 Moved to Shanghai, China

1926 Off to San Francisco, CA, Opened Temple of Heaven

1929 Stock Market crashed; Depression

1930 Daughter Margot Rosaly born.

1934 Went bankrupt; moved to Beverly Hills

1936 Opened Gift Shop in Beverly Hills Hotel

1938 Otto Wiesinger returned to Germany

1940 Edith married Julius Gilbert

1950 Moved store to Beverly Drive

1952 Margot married

1954 Ethel Became citizen

1954 Closed store; obtained real estate license

1957 Visited Europe, Israel

1967 Moved to Charlevoix, MI

1984 Deceased, age 94

Charlevoix Courier

Ethel Wiesinger, 94

Ethel Wiesinger, 94, of Charlevoix, died unexpectedly May 15, 1984, at Charlevoix Area Hospital.

Arrangements are being handled by Winchester Funeral Home in Charlevoix and funeral time and place will be announced tomorrow.

The former Ethel Liebman was born March 23, 1890 in Czernowitz, Austria-Hungary. In 1916, she married

Ethel Wiesinger

Otto Wiesinger, originally from Hamburg, West Germany, in New York City. Mr. Wiesinger preceded her in death in the early 1950s.

Mrs. Wiesinger traveled extensively with her parents and husband and lived for a number of years in China. Much of her life was spent in California where she operated gift shops at the Beverly Hills Hotel and the St. Francis Hotel in San Francisco, Calif.

In 1967, Mrs. Wiesinger moved to Charlevoix. She was active in the Congregational Church, the Charlevoix Women's Club and the German Conversation Group. She was currently teaching a German class at the Petoskey Friendship Center.

Although she had only nine years of formal schooling, Mrs. Wiesinger had a tremendous intellect and wisdom. She was an avid reader and believed that history held many valuable lessons. She often commented that life is a school and every day is a school day. Mrs. Wiesinger was actively learning from people and from reading books, mainly relating to history, until the day of her death.

According to her friend Sally Scholl, Mrs. Wiesinger often would say, "I try to accept people as they are, not like I would like them to be, or think they should be." With this philosophy, Mrs. Wiesinger succeeded in making each person she met feel special.

Survivors include two daughters, Edith Gilbert of Charlevoix and Dr. Margot Smith of Berkley, Calif.; four grandchildren, Walter, Peter, Larry and Janet; and countless friends and admirers.

The family suggests memorials to the Julius Gilbert Scholrship Fund at the Charlevoix Area Hospital or to the Crooked Tree Arts Council in Petoskey.

Marriage Certificate
Ethel Liebman and Otto Wiesinger

This Certifies

that OTTO WIESINGER,

of NEW YORK CITY, N. Y.

and ETHEL LIEBMANN,

of NEW YORK CITY, N. Y.

WERE UNITED IN

MARRIAGE

ACCORDING TO

the Ordinance of GOD and the Laws of

The State of New Jersey

on the SECOND day of SEPTEMBER in the year One Thousand Nine Hundred and SIXTEEN.

Witnesses: *Arthur Devries.*

Elly Devries

Adolph C. Carstin
RECORDER,
HOBOKEN, N. J.

Ethel Liebman Wiesinger, U. S. Citizen, 1954

*To her dismay, Ethel Liebman Wiesinger was denied citizenship during WWII partly because her native Czernowitz was at times occupied by either Allied or Axis countries: the USSR, Germany, Poland, and Romania. She was also compromised, she felt unfairly, by her privately showing gift shop merchandise to Leni Riefenstahl, a filmmaker famous for her Nazi propaganda film of the 1936 Olympics, **Triumph of the Will,** who was staying at the Beverly Hills Hotel. After finally receiving her citizenship in 1954, she travelled to Europe and Israel to visit family.*

Biographisches Handbuch des deutschen Auswärtigen Dienstes

1871-1945

Wiesinger, Otto

* 14. 1.1885 Waldsassen
† 3. 6.1956 Bad Pyrmont

ev.-luth.

Eltern: Karl Georg W., bayer. Oberregierungsrat, Reichsbevollmächtigter für Zölle und Steuern; Anna Franziska geb. Walther

∞ I. 1916 Ethel geb. Liebman; II. Edith geb. Winter; III. Gertrud geb. Winter

Kinder aus I. Ehe: Edith (2.9.1917), Margot (27.8.1930)

Gymnasium; kaufmännische Ausbildung; dann bis 1914 Tätigkeit für Firmen der Farbenindustrie in Shanghai; 1914 Militärdienst in Tsingtau, dann in japan. Kriegsgefangenschaft; seit 1916 Wohnsitz in New York, seit 1919 selbständiger Im- und Exportkaufmann in Shanghai, seit Ende der 1920er Jahre Wohnsitz in den USA, Händler für orientalische Kunst in San Francisco, seit 1936 in Los Angeles, seit 1937 in New York; 1940 bis 1942 Tätigkeit für das DNB in New York, seit 1942 beim Deutschen Verlag in Berlin.

6. 4.1943	DA AA, Wissenschaftlicher Hilfsarbeiter, Nachrichten- und Presseabt., Ref. P.gen./Organisations- und Verwaltungsangelegenheiten, Personalien, Verbreitung der dt. Presse im Ausland, seit Dez. 1943 in der Ausweichstelle des AA in Hohenelbe/Riesengebirge
5.10.1944	Militärdienst

Später Wohnsitz in Berlin, dann in Hamburg.

Nachlass im Archiv der Hoover Institution in Stanford/Kalifornien.

Biographical Handbook of
Germans with Outstanding Service,
1871-1945

Wiesinger, Otto
Born Jan. 14, 1885 Waldsassen;
Died Jun. 3, 1956 Bad Pyrmont
Parents: Karl Georg W. Bavaria.
> Council of The High Government;
>> authority, customs and taxes;
> **Anna Franziska** nee Walter.

Married:
> I. 1916 Ethel nee Liebman;
> II Edith nee Winter.
> III Gertrude nee Winter.
> Children of Ethel:
>> Edith, Sept 2, 1917;
>> Margot Aug 27, 1930.

Gymnasium (college):
Business training;
  in 1914 employed by companies in the dye industry in Shanghai;
  1914 Military Service in Tsingtau, then in Japanese captivity.
  In 1916 resided in New York;
  in 1916 self employed as an export businessman in Shanghai;
  to the end of 1920 lived in the USA as an Oriental art importer in
        San Francisco;
  in 1936 Los Angeles
  in 1937, New York;
  1940 until 1942 active for the DNB, Deutsches Nachrichtenbüro,
        Nazi German news agency in New York;
  in 1942 for a German publisher in Berlin.
  April 6, 1943. Communications specialist for a news and press
        agency for disseminating news abroad;
  in 1943 to the Hohenelbe Riesengebirge region.
  Oct. 5, 1944 Military service.
Later lived in Berlin and Hamburg.

His letters and papers are found at the Hoover Institute, Stanford.

Otto Wiesinger

Otto Wiesinger (1885-1956) and Ethel Liebman (1890-1984) married in 1916. He was an entrepreneur who sought to make his fortune buying and selling through various international ventures.

A German citizen, he was profoundly influenced by the political and economic events of his time. In 1914 he fought in Germany's war against Japan in the Siege of Tsingtau (China) and later supported a failed Chinese warlord, Zhang Zuolin. In San Francisco during the 1930s Great Depression he went bankrupt. He remained loyal to Germany; in 1938 he returned to Nazi Germany to support Hitler.

At the age of 59 during WWII he was drafted into the German army where he worked in communications. After the war he lived in Berlin when it was isolated by the USSR and survived the Berlin Air Lift. He married three times.

He left the family when I was six so I did not know him very well. In 1954 my sister Edith and I visited him in Hamburg, Germany, where he was working as a translator. He died two years later.

Margot W. Smith
2021

Otto Wiesinger
Death Certificate, 1956

Sterbeurkunde

(Standesamt **B a d   P y r m o n t** - - - Nr. **142/1956** ,

Der Kaufmann Otto Karl Georg Christof **W i e s i n g e r**

- - - - - - - - - - - - - **evangelisch-lutherisch** -

wohnhaft **in Hamburg 26, Grießstraße 85** - - - - - - - ,

ist am **3. Juli 1956** - - - - - um **9** Uhr **45** Minuten

in **Bad Pyrmont, im Krankenhaus Sankt Georg** - -verstorben.

D **er** Verstorbene war geboren am **14. Januar 1885** - - - - -

in **Waldsassen, Kreis Bayreuth** - - - - - - - - - -

(Standesamt **Waldsassen** - - - - - - - - Nr. **3/1885** -)

Vater **Karl Georg Wiesinger, zuletzt wohnhaft in Altona**

- -

Mutter **Anna Franziska, geborene Walther, zuletzt** - -

wohnhaft in Waldsassen - - - - - - - - - - -

D **er** Verstorbene war — ~~nicht~~ — verheiratet **mit der Gertrud** -

Margarete Elfriede Wiesinger, geborene Winter - - -

- -

Bad Pyrmont , den **4. Juli 1956**

Der Standesbeamte

(Siegel)

In Vertretung: I.A.

Bestell-Nr. 6/233 Sterbeurkunde G 1
Vordruckverlag für die Standesämter Heinrich Buschmann, Münster (Westf.) 28. 4. 56 40 mm

Petoskey News Review
Edith Gilbert, 91

August 3, 2009

Charlevoix's 'Grand Dame' leaves legacy
of tenacity and generosity

Christina Rohn News-Review Staff Writer

Those who knew Edith Gilbert called her extraordinary - those who loved her called her an inspiration. "It occurs to me that she was part Julia Child, part Perle Mesta and part Emily Post - all together, an original," said Suzy Farbman, author, journalist, and long-time friend of Gilbert's. "There are many of us who considered her a real anchor in our lives, and we'll miss her greatly."

Gilbert, a long-time resident of Charlevoix, and world-renowned author, wedding consultant and etiquette legend, died Friday morning at Charlevoix Hospital at the age of 91. Gilbert's nephew, Larry Smith, said his aunt suffered a heart attack just two days before, but didn't let that slow her down. "She was alert, awake and active through the whole thing," he said. "Her last official act was to have cinnamon buns sent to a friend."

Family and friends say this was just like Gilbert to be caring, compassionate and giving until the very end. Often called the "Grand Dame" of Charlevoix, Gilbert was the epitome of class, throwing numerous galas and celebrations for family, friends and acquaintances. She was also a philanthropist.

In the early '60s she became an original member of the Friends of the Charlevoix Public Library, and worked to establish the Charlevoix Waterfront Art Fair. She was also a board member for the Charlevoix Historical Society, volunteer for the Charlevoix Area Hospital and responsible for the current railings on the drawbridge in downtown Charlevoix.

In the '70s, she became a founding member of the Crooked Tree Arts Center, where in 2002, she was honored by having a gallery named after her. Liz Ahrens, executive director for the Crooked Tree Arts Center, described Gilbert as a force. "Wherever she was in a crowd, she'd have a great sparkle in her eye and a giggle that was tremendous," she said. Ahrens said Gilbert was a great supporter of the arts wherever she went. "Edith was a crucial part of the arts center all the way along ... if she was on your side, you could never think of a better ally," she said.

For Ken Winter, former editor of the Petoskey News-Review and his wife Ginger - Gilbert was their matchmaker. Ken said Gilbert was not subtle when she wanted to introduce people. "One day she came into the News-Review and barricaded the door, and said 'Have you called (Ginger) yet?' and I said, 'No,' then she said, 'You'd better call her right now,'" he said, laughing as he recalled the incident. Winter did make the call, and eventually, when he and Ginger married, Gilbert served as the couple's matron of honor. "She played our cupid, and every Valentine's Day, we'd always send her a Valentine's card," Ginger said.

When it came to cards, Gilbert enjoyed receiving, but she also enjoyed sharing her humor in the form of holiday greetings. "Every year we'd get a Christmas card with Edith on the front, wearing the same Christmas sweater, doing something preposterous and age inappropriate - she was always in some new adventure," Farbman said. "She never really thought she was old, she was always a dynamo."

Gilbert was born in New York City, N.Y., on Sept. 2, 1917, to Ethel (Liebman) and Otto Wiesinger. After World Ward I, her family moved to Germany; then to Shanghai, China, for four years; and to San Francisco, CA., in 1927, where her parents were in the import/export business. In 1935, her family moved to Beverly Hills, CA., where her mother ran the gift shop at the Beverly Hills Hotel, featuring imported ceramics and art. . Her sister, Margot, was born in 1930 in San Francisco.

Edith met her future husband, Julius, at the Beverly Hills Hotel in 1939. He proposed at the Hollywood Brown Derby, and they married and moved to Arden Park in Detroit in 1940. During World War II, Gilbert worked for the war bond campaign, and was a driver for the American Red Cross motor pool.For much of this time, the couple summered in Charlevoix, and in 1963, made the decision to move there permanently.

In the early '70s, Gilbert became a columnist for the Charlevoix Courier, which then turned into a column for the Petoskey News-Review. She has also written for the Detroit Free Press and various magazines. Her work has been featured in the New York Times, Chicago Tribune and United Feature Syndicate.

As an author, Edith wrote several books including "The Complete Wedding Planner," the historically significant "Summer Resort Life: Tango, Teas and All," as well as "All About Parties" and "Let's Set the Table." She also worked as a wedding consultant, spoke about wedding etiquette, and made a video documentary of her slide presentation on the history of table settings titled "When Eating Became Dining."

In 1993, in Charlevoix she saw that the new drawbridge railings were unsafe for children crossing the bridge and not aesthetically consistent with Charlevoix's image. She petitioned the state and corresponded with eight engineers over the next two years to have new, safer and more beautiful railings installed on Charlevoix's drawbridge. These are the current railings.At age 85, she embraced the Internet by setting up a Web site, edithgilbert.com, which allowed her to advise brides and grooms around the world. Sometimes whimsical, often serious, Edith always wrote to stir debate of the important issues of both local and national interest.

At the young age of 89, Gilbert tried a new venture by designing, manufacturing and distributing "Plum Crazy," a plum conserve, to more than 30 gift and gourmet shops throughout Northern Michigan. "She was a marketing guru ... if she was selling her Plum Crazy, she would be wearing her plum colored outfit," Ahrens said.

Friends of Gilbert said she was like a chameleon, always reinventing herself. "I was astounded at how she maintained being vital and relevant right up until the end," Farbman said. "As my husband said, she was interesting and interested, Charlevoix will never be the same."

Melissa Keiswetter, a long-time friend of Gilbert's, said Edith touched her life in many ways. "She's been a mother figure, mentor and a very best friend," she said. "I would say, of all the people in my life, I have learned more from Edith Gilbert ... she has made me a greater person than I would have been before meeting her."

Ginger Winter said she is still trying to grasp the concept of Gilbert's passing. "I can't believe she's not on the planet," she said. "A life without Edith is going to be weird for a while."

Smith said his aunt had a profound effect on everyone she came in contact with. "She was quite witty and charming ... everybody loved to be in her presence," he said. "She was a light and a wonderful woman - we thought she'd live forever."

Gilbert's family will be hosting a memorial service in her honor 11 a.m., Thursday, Aug. 6, at the Crooked Tree Arts Center in Petoskey. Contributions in Gilbert's name can be made to the Crooked Tree Arts Council, 461 Mitchell Street, Petoskey, Mich., 49770; the Charlevoix Area Hospital Foundation, 14700 Lake Shore Dr., Charlevoix, Mich., 49720, or to a charity of your choice.

"(Gilbert) had a long, fantastic life, and we're trying to celebrate that," Smith said.For more information about Gilbert, and her work, visit her Web site, at www.edithgilbert.com.

Edith is survived by her sister, Margot Smith, niece, Janet (Smith) Linney, nephews, Walter, Peter and Larry Smith, six grandnieces and -nephews. She is also survived by her stepson, Jay Gilbert and his wife, Vicky, their three children, Jennifer (Gilbert) Duffy, Vicci (Gilbert) Duca, Curtis Gilbert, six grandchildren, and numerous great-grandchildren.

Charlevoix
Courier

Julius W. Gilbert, 81

Julius W. Gilbert, 81, of Charlevoix, died April 10, 1984, at Charlevoix Area Hospital.

Private memorial services will be held at a later date.

Born in Kalamazoo on July 23, 1902, Mr. Gilbert graduated from Detroit University School in Grosse Pointe. He joined the D.W.G. Cigar Co. and served on the board of directors until his retirement.

During World War II, he was appointed a Dollar-a-Year Man to the U.S. Treasury Department and promoted the sale of war bonds for the state of Michigan.

With several associates, he built The Lodge of Charlevoix in 1962, which he sold to his longtime friend and manager, Jack Uhrick, in October 1979.

Mr. Gilbert was a member of the board of directors of the Charlevoix Area Hospital for nine years, 1965-1974, and was active in all the fundraising campaigns for the hospital.

He was an avid golfer in his youth and won the Northern State Championship in 1921 and also played in an exhibition golf match for the Petoskey-Bay View Country Club.

His interest in speedboat racing won him numerous trophies, including the Harbor Springs First Annual Water Carnival Trophy in 1927, with a Hacker designed speedboat which was the fastest boat on the Great Lakes at that time.

Among his many hobbies, he enjoyed hunting and fishing.

When he moved to Charlevoix permanently, after being a summer resident since 1910, he built a studio in his home where he enjoyed carving wooden animals out of mahogany, ebony and walnut. His work was exhibited at the Charlevoix Waterfront Art Fair and recently at the Virginia McCune Arts Center in October 1983.

Mr. Gilbert is survived by his wife, Edith Wiesinger Gilbert, whom he married at Santa Monica, Calif., April 9, 1940; a daughter, Patricia Grove of New Haven, Conn.; a son, Jay, of Rochester, N.Y.; six grandchildren; one great-granddaughter.

The family suggests memorials to the Julius Gilbert Medical Scholarship Fund at the Charlevoix Area Hospital, or to the Crooked Tree Arts Council in Petoskey.

Karl Wiesinger Title Page
The Duties and Taxes of the German Nation
His design for collecting customs in Hamburg harbor became a model for U. S. customs in 1812,

Die Zölle und Steuern

des Deutschen Reiches.

———

Nach dem jetzigen Stande der Gesetzgebung
vollständig neu bearbeitet

von

Karl Wiesinger,

K. b. Oberregierungsrat, Reichsbevollmächtigter für Zölle und Steuern
in Altona.

6. Auflage.

1912.
München und Berlin.
J. Schweitzer Verlag (Arthur Sellier).

Wiesinger, Karl.
Die Zölle Und Steuern Des Deutschen Reiches.
(The Duties and Taxes of the German Nation),
6.Aufl. München: J. Schweitzer (A. Sellier), 1912

Photogaph Listing

www.ingramcontent.com/pod-product-compliance
Lightning Source LLC
Chambersburg PA
CBHW051756050726
47598CB00006B/2307